Just Show Me
Which Button to Click!

Just Show Me
Which Button to Click!

in POWERPOINT®
2007

PEGGY DUNCAN

PRESS

Atlanta, Georgia

Just Show Me Which Button to Click! in PowerPoint 2007

ISBN: 978-0-9674728-8-1

Library of Congress Control Number: 2010936889

Book layout done in Microsoft® Word 2007.

Author photo by McCollum Photography, Atlanta, GA, www.MccPhoto.com.
Cover design by High Profile Studio, Atlanta, GA, www.HighProfileStudio.com.

Trademarks
Windows, PowerPoint, Excel, and Microsoft are registered trademarks of Microsoft® Corporation. Screen shots reprinted by permission from Microsoft Corporation. Any other products or trademarks mentioned belong to their respective companies.

Companies, names, and/or data used in screens and sample output are fictitious unless otherwise noted.

FAMILY

PEACE

LOVE

Acknowledgments

I did it to my family again. I sat down to write this book, and everything else was forgotten. But people who love me understand, and they continue to put up with me! I LOVE you guys, and I appreciate your staying on me about getting up from the computer to eat, exercise, and drink more water.

Contacting the Author

If you have a request, comment, or testimonial for this book, Peggy Duncan looks forward to hearing from you.

Connect at worksmart@PeggyDuncan.com or call 404-492-8197 Eastern.

www.DigitalBreakThroughs.com
The Digital Breakthroughs Institute
Atlanta GA
Technology and Productivity Training Open to the Public
Founder, Peggy Duncan

www.PeggyDuncan.com
Join Peggy's Private Email List
Receive free timesaving tips and eNewsletter

www.SUITEMinute.com
Peggy's Award-Winning Technology Blog
Technology tips that make work easier

www.Facebook.com/DigitalBreakThroughs
Facebook Fan Page - Join for free

www.Twitter.com/**peggyduncan**
Follow Peggy on Twitter

www.YouTube.com/**digitalbreakthroughs**
YouTube Channel with How-To Videos

" " What People Are Saying About Peggy Duncan

As always, your seminar is chock full of information and tips I can apply today
that will save time, effort, and frustration ~ not to mention reduce my stress level!"
Katherine Swartz
Greater Atlanta Home Builders Association

"The tips and tricks I received in this half-day seminar will save me many hours of time."
Steve Bistritz

"Peggy is a wonderfully vibrant instructor. She presents the information in a concise,
understandable manner. I love taking her seminars because I always learn
new tips and shortcuts that I can use immediately."
Michelle Y., BearingPoint

"Your presentations are as outstanding as your books!"
Janette Pierce

"Thanks sooooo much for sharing your data-bank of knowledge. We need more trainers
like you who give added value at each of your sessions!!"
Dr. Marcia Riley, EA, Inc.
www.writingforresults.com

"Based upon the number of tips I took away with me, it was time well spent AND
I'm going to the next one, too."
Thomas R. Baley

"I am a consultant and therefore lost revenues to attend the seminar. It was worth every
penny and minute of time. I have already seen the benefit. Peggy is a wonderful presenter.
This should be a must for each executive's tool box."
Robin Hensley, www.personalconstruction.com

"Worth every penny. The software I've been using all this time is now worth so much
more to me-not to mention the hours I'll save. Thank you, thank you."
Chris Coleman

"Great job! Excellent, energetic, and interesting!"
Camille Goodlett, Fulton County Economic Development

"I learned tips that will save me time in doing proposals and price quotes. I was looking
to have this outsourced, but now I can save the money and do it myself."
Evelyn Arnette
A Customer's Point of View

TABLE OF CONTENTS

Introduction

Do you want to create presentations that are more than just boring bullets? If so, don't put this book on a shelf to collect dust. It's not for your nightstand either. *Just Show Me Which Button to Click! in PowerPoint 2007* will help you create more time for planning a presentation instead of working on it.

Who Is This Book For?

Just Show Me Which Button to Click! in PowerPoint 2007 is for busy people who are already computer savvy. You could be new to PowerPoint, or you may have been using it for years but not taking advantage of some of its best features. This documentation does not cover the Mac format.

How Content is Arranged

I've mostly introduced commands based on how they fall on the ribbon, but sometimes not. I've included screenshots as a visual when I thought you'd need more explanation.

Writing Style

You won't see any fluff in this book. I have a habit of not taking ten pages to express something I can say in a paragraph. You'll notice throughout that I get right to the point. If the heading explains what the text is about, I don't waste words re-explaining it. When it's obvious that you need to click OK until you're back out of a dialog box, I don't say it.

Formatting

In most cases, the **bold** text in an instruction is the action you should take—what you click. At times, you'll notice that some instructions will stop before you finish the task. This is because the next step should be obvious to you (e.g., click **OK**).

For commands that would require a lot more explanation, I've added links to video demos on my Website. I've indicated this throughout the book. Visit www.DigitalBreakthroughs.com/ppttutor.htm.

The 🔊 symbol indicates a special point. Don't ignore these!

notes

GETTING READY

You should spend a few minutes examining the new PowerPoint window. Learn where each element is because I'll refer to them throughout the book.

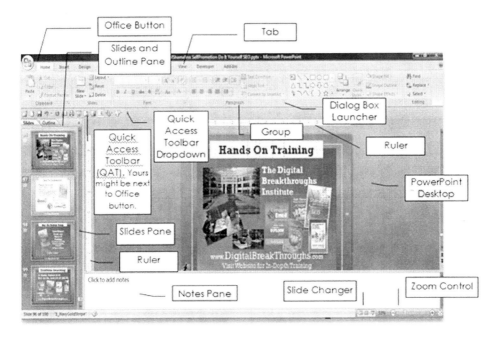

For this training, please ensure you have the following options activated.

1. Open PowerPoint. The Slides Pane on the left is where you can create text on your slide (click **Outline** tab). The actual slide is on the right. You'll see dotted boxes on a slide called placeholders. The Notes Pane under the slide is where you can click and type speaker notes. You can also print these notes to

refer to during your presentation (or you can view your notes during your slide show, page 99). Various task panes will appear later.

2. Display the ruler. Click the **View** tab, tick **Ruler** (in the **Show/Hide** group).

3. Increase the number of undos to **100.** Click the **Office button, PowerPoint Options** (bottom of dialog box), **Advanced.** Change the **Maximum number of undos** to **100.**

In an open presentation, you can always click the Undo button to work backwards to undo a mistake. When you make a mess, 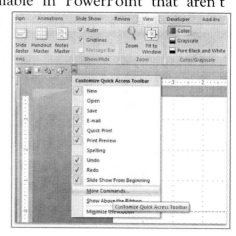 click the Undo or Redo buttons located on the Quick Access Toolbar. Click the drop-down box and undo up to 100 steps before or after closing the document.

When you want to undo more than one step, click the drop-down box, and point the mouse over each one to highlight them, then click. You can also click the Redo button to go back and forth. You can't skip around steps.

Customize the Quick Access Toolbar

There are many commands available in PowerPoint that aren't visible by default. Once you start using the software, you'll discover what you need quick access to. Here's how to customize the Quick Access Toolbar (QAT).

1. Click the Customize Quick Access Toolbar drop-down button (or right-click anywhere on the toolbar), and click **More Commands.**

2. The PowerPoint Options box will open. On the left, **Customize** should be highlighted. On the right side under *Choose commands from*, choose **All Commands**.

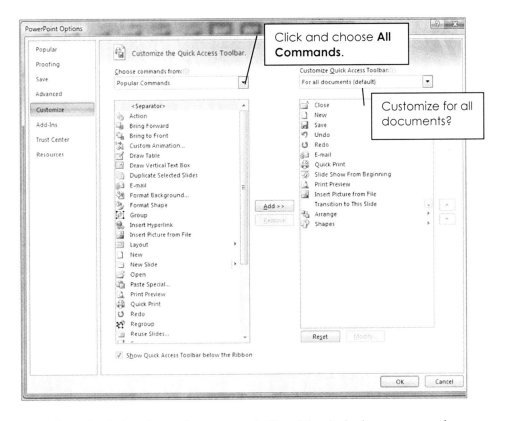

3. Scroll to find the desired command. Double-click the command to move to the right side, click **OK**. To rearrange the order of how these commands appear on the Quick Access Toolbar, click the up/down buttons on the far right.

4. Choose whether to customize the toolbar for all documents or only for the one you're working in (see box next to All Commands).

File Extensions

PowerPoint uses the following file extensions in your file structure: .pptx is a PowerPoint presentation; .potx is a PowerPoint template; and .ppsx is a PowerPoint Show, .thmx is a theme. You'll learn more about these later in this book.

Page Setup

Click the **Design** tab, **Page Setup**. This is where you'll choose the:

▤ Type of presentation you're creating (e.g., On-screen show).

▤ Width and height of page/slide (margins).

▤ Page number you want your slides to begin with.

▤ Page orientation for slides and notes, either landscape or portrait. You can't mix orientations in one presentation. If you need to switch to a slide with a different orientation, create a hyperlink to it. To make sure you can get back, create a hyperlink on the other slide back to the first one (see more on creating hyperlinks on page 82).

Ways to View Your Slides

You can change how you view your slides by clicking the **View** tab and clicking a command in the Presentation Views group. .

Normal. You'll see the Outline and Slides tabs on the left side of the window; the Slides Pane in the middle where you'll add text and or change the design and animations; and the Notes Pane at the bottom to add any speaker notes.

Slide Sorter. You can view all the slides in your presentation at once. You can move slides around, add transitions, hide, and delete from this view.

Notes Pages. If you've added any speaker notes to a slide, you'll see them here.

Slide Show. See how your presentation looks in Show mode. During the show, click anywhere on your monitor or hit the Spacebar to advance the slides. Press **Esc** when finished.

Master Views. You'll use the Slide Master, Handout Master, and Notes Master to add information and designs you want to appear consistently on each slide. More details on this topic will be covered later in this lesson.

The Slide Changer

You can also change the views by using the **Slide Changer.** The Slide Changer allows you to change views quickly with a single mouse click (it's located at the bottom of your screen, right-hand side).

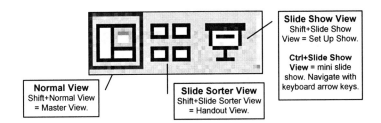

The Slide Changer includes the Normal and Slide Sorter views as previously discussed. You can also click to start a slide show from the current slide.

📢 *Press F5 on the keyboard to launch your slide show from the beginning. To start a slide show from the current slide, press **Shift+F5.***

If you hold down your **Shift** key and point to each icon on the Slide Changer, you'll see how to display other views (Slide Master view, Handout Master view, Set Up Show. You'll learn more about these views later.) If you hold down the **Ctrl** key and click **Slide Show from current slide**, a mini slide show will launch (press **Esc** to end).

Zoom

There are several ways to zoom in on a slide.

1. Click the **View** menu, **Zoom**, and make your selection.
2. Use the Zoom slider to the right of the Slide Changer.
3. Use the wheel on your mouse (if yours has one). Hold down the **Ctrl** key as you roll the wheel up or down (you can also use your mouse wheel on Web sites, other documents, etc.).

Insert, Move, Resize Objects

📢 *In PowerPoint, an object is a table, chart, graphic, equation, shape, or other form of information.*

Your mouse pointer takes on several different shapes depending on the job you need it to do. You can use the mouse pointer to resize and move your graphic.

1. Resize a graphic by selecting it first, then hold your mouse pointer over any one of the *corner selection handles* that appear. The pointer will turn into a 2-headed arrow. Click and drag it to resize the graphic. A **2-headed arrow is used to RESIZE.**
2. Move a graphic by holding the mouse pointer anywhere over it until it turns into a 4-headed arrow. Click and drag to move the graphic. Or you can use your keyboard arrow keys to move it. A **4-headed arrow is used to MOVE.**

Nudge Objects

You can use the keyboard arrow keys to move objects. Select the object you want to move. Use your keyboard arrow keys to move it in any direction. Each press of the key will move the object one grid unit (which is based on the default or whatever you changed it to).

📢 *To nudge an object in even smaller increments, hold down the **Ctrl** key as you press the keyboard arrow keys. If the object appears to jump and refuses to nudge the way you want, see Align Using the Grid on page 38.*

Selecting Objects

Throughout this book, you'll have to select an object before you can do something with it. There are several ways to do this.

- Select an object that is very tiny or possibly hidden from view, you can select any object on the slide, then **Tab** to select others.

- Select more than one object on the slide, then hold down the **Shift key** as you click each one.

- Select many objects on a slide at one time by using your mouse to drag it across all the objects. When you release the mouse, you'll see selection boxes on each object that is selected. If you missed one, hold down the Shift key and click it.

- Use the Selection and Visibility Pane (more on page 37).

DESIGNING AND CREATING

THEMES

Design templates in previous versions of PowerPoint have been replaced by themes. Click the **Design** tab. Each theme includes an organized collection of colors, fonts, and effects with a matching background, all of which were developed by a team of professional designers.

Apply a Built-In Theme

Once you choose a theme on the **Design** tab, click the **More** button for additional choices. Next to the More button are commands that allow you to apply optional colors, font choices, and effects. Everything has been carefully coordinated to match, so it's a good idea to use these built-in choices (unless your company has specific colors you must use).

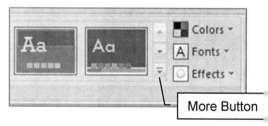

More Button

You can review the themes before you apply by running your mouse over them. Click the one you want to use (you can change it later). To select another color palette, click the Theme **Colors** drop-down box and choose.

Create a Custom Theme

If your company or organization has pre-defined colors you must use, check first to see if they've already added a template to your templates folder (refer to information on templates beginning on page 10).

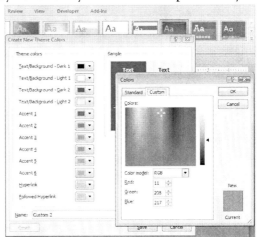

You can create your own custom colors.

1. Click the **Design** tab, the **Colors** drop-down box (located in the Themes group), **Create New Theme Colors**.

2. Click the drop-down box next to each design element and either choose a pre-defined color (or click More Colors if you need to create your own colors).

3. On the **Custom** tab, type the RGB colors that match your organization's color mandate.

To choose a different font set, click the **Fonts** drop-down box. And for a particular effect you'd like for your graphics, click the **Effects** drop-down box (this makes slight changes to the smoothness of your graphic edges. You'll have to have a graphic on the slide to see the changes.

◄ᵈᵎ You can apply your custom theme to Word and Excel documents (under their Page Setup tab).

Save a Theme

If you customize a theme, you can save it and apply it to other presentations, Word documents, and Excel spreadsheets. To save your theme, click the **Design** tab. Click the **More** button (see the figure on page 8 for help locating this button), **Save Current Theme** (the .thmx file extension). You'll save your custom theme to the **Document Themes** folder, giving it a logical name.

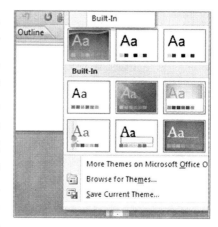

📢 *You can email a .thmx file to others.*

Apply Your Custom Theme

Once you've saved your custom theme, you can use it in subsequent presentations. Click the **Design** tab, **More** button. Your theme should be under **Custom**. RIGHT-click on it, and choose how to apply it.

📢 *If you don't want to Apply to All Slides, click the thumbnails in the Slides pane (or go to Slide Sorter view), and select slides you want to apply the theme to, click the **More** button, and choose **Apply to Selected Slides**.*

THE MASTER TEMPLATE

You can save a lot of time by creating a template that has a pre-designed theme, design elements, and slides you use repeatedly. In this scenario, you'll create a new document, save it as a template, and design it from the master. On the master, you'll apply a theme and add common elements that you want to appear on all slides, such as a company logo. Then back in the presentation, you can add common slides such as a contact page.

For example, you have various products you sell to different markets. You want your PowerPoint presentations to have a consistent design for all products. You'll create a new presentation, choose a theme and customize it if you need to. You want the product photo to appear on the left with the description on the right. You also want your company logo to appear on every slide in the footer along with your Web address.

You can set all this up once with a template, and reuse it by creating new presentations based on a copy of it.

Slide Master

The style elements for the font and paragraph styles and the position and alignment of titles, text, and footers all reside in the master. If you want to change any of this for the majority or all of your slides, you should do so from the Slide Master View. Consequently, any new slide you add will reflect these changes. (You can change individual slides later if you need to.)

You can create multiple slide masters and apply a different theme to each one.

Slide Layout and Placeholders

To create a new presentation, click the **New** button on the Quick Access Toolbar (or press Ctrl+N). A slide will appear in Normal view, with a layout and two placeholders. Layouts specify the overall arrangement of slide content, and placeholders (surrounded by boxes with dotted lines as the border) represent individual pieces of data you can rearrange. The text inside the placeholder is there to act as a reminder of what to do (e.g., "Click to add title"). You can change an instruction in the placeholder on the master, but none of it will print. You can also insert additional placeholders (page 16) on the master.

Built-In Templates

PowerPoint 2007 comes packed with pre-designed templates with a more professional finish than previous versions. Their Website offers even more. When you click the **Office** button, **New, Installed Templates**, also click to see the various templates available on the Microsoft Web site, everything from an envelope to certificates. Double-click whatever you want to use.

◀)) *If you're on a company network, instead of clicking Installed Templates, you might see General and Presentation tabs. Click each of these tabs to find more templates.*

Create Your Own Template

You can design a slide once and save it as a template to reuse later.

1. Click the **New** button on the Quick Access Toolbar (or press **Ctrl+N**).

2. Save this document as a template. Click the **Office** button, **Save As**, give your template a descriptive name so you'll recognize it later.

3. Under **Save as type**, click to change the document type to **PowerPoint Template** (which is the **.potx** extension). PowerPoint

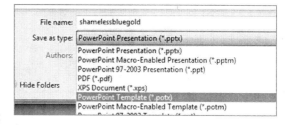

will navigate to the Presentation Templates folder automatically.

4. **Save** the file as you normally would (either in a current folder, create a new folder, or just save as it is). Continue working on your new template.

You can make your design template the default simply by naming it blank.potx. It'll become the default design PowerPoint uses when you create new presentations.

Design from the Master

At this point, you're working inside your saved template. Next, you'll go to the slide master to apply a theme and add common elements you want to apply on all slides such as changing the placement of the slide #, adding your company logo, etc.

1. Click the **View** tab, **Slide Master**. Thumbnails of the available layouts appear in the Slides pane on the left (if you don't see this pane, hover your mouse over the far left edge of your screen until it turns into a double arrow, and drag. The first slide is the main master layout. Don't get confused by all this. For now, concentrate on this top thumbnail and ignore the rest.

   When you see this type of placeholders and text, you know you're in Slide Master view.

   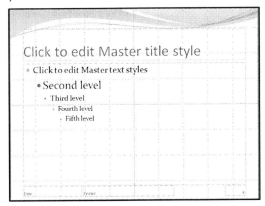

2. Apply a theme to your template, either one of the built-in options or one you've created (see information on themes beginning on page 8).

3. In the Slides/Outline pane, click the first thumbnail slide (the Slide Master).

4. On the master slide, delete the date/time text box (click any border one time to select it, press the **Delete** key). I'm deleting this now because when I work with the header/footer, I'm going to deselect the option for this to appear.

5. Click any border of the footer box, and drag it to the left margin, perfectly aligned with the main placeholder (I usually put my Web address in the footer. I'll show you how to do that later. Don't type presentation text on your master.

You can change how the text is aligned in the placeholders. For example, if you want the footer text to be centered, select the footer placeholder, and press **Ctrl+E**. For now, leave it left-aligned (shortcut is **Ctrl+L**).

If you want the slide number (#) to place somewhere else, drag it there. For example, to the right margin. (To drag it, hold your mouse over its placeholder border. When the pointer turns into a **4-headed arrow**, click and drag to desired location.)

Add a Background

Your theme will have background styles already built-in. Click, **Background Styles** (located on the **Design** tab in the Background group), and click one that appears.

If none of these appeal to you, click **Format Background** for more Fill options (you'll see more information on Fill when you're ready to work on your title slide, page 19. If you want to add a picture to your background, see how on page 20).

Add Your Logo

While you're still working with the Slide Master, add your organization logo so it'll appear on each slide. Click the **Insert** tab, **Picture**. Double-click it to insert it, resize, and drag it to the desired location.

If your logo has a white box around it, make it transparent (see page 30).

Change the Header and Footer

You'll probably have some information that needs to appear on every slide (such as your Web site address or slide number). The Header and Footer command makes this easy.

1. Continuing from the previous lesson, press **Ctrl+S** to save all the work you've done so far (you're still working inside the master). Click the **Insert** tab, **Header & Footer** (located in the Text group). On the **Slide** tab:

   ▣ Don't want date/time to appear, so untick the box. I've already deleted its placeholder.

   ▣ Want slide number to print on each slide, so tick the box.

   ▣ Want company Web site address to appear on each slide in Footer placeholder, so tick the **Footer** box, and click inside the text box and type it (or whatever text you want to appear). If you don't add it here, it won't appear as part of the master.

◻ Don't want this information to show on title slide, so tick the **Don't show on title slide** box.

2. While you're still in the Header and Footer dialog box, click the **Notes and Handouts** tab. For this example, do the following:

◻ Untick the **Date and time** box.

◻ Type your name and work title in the **Header** box. Use the spacebar to add some space between them.

◻ Tick the **Footer** box, and click inside the text box and type your company Web site address, space over and type your phone number, space over and type your email address.

🔊 *Later, when you create handouts for your presentation, this information will appear on the printed pages (and on your Notes). You can also create your handout in Word for more header and footer placement options.*

3. Tick **Don't show on title slide** (because you'll want to have more flexibility when deciding where to place objects on this slide).

4. Click Apply to All.

🔊 *If you look at your slides outside of the master, no text will appear until you add slides to your presentation.*

Add Additional Placeholders

If you ever need to, you can create additional placeholders for different kinds of text and objects. Go to the Slide Master and click **Insert Placeholder** (located in the Master Layout group), and click the desired format. Click on the slide, and drag to draw the placeholder.

🔊 *You can only add placeholders to a master slide.*

Format Text

The font and bullet style and color are part of your theme. Unless your organization has special fonts and colors you should use, it's a good idea to keep your theme as is. Remember, professional designers worked with this version of PowerPoint and selected these combinations.

While still working from the master, you'll make adjustments to things such as the alignment of the heading text in a placeholder, different shapes, sizes, and colors for each bullet level, and so on. Because you're working from the master, you won't have to make the same changes on every new slide.

The following is for example only. You should still be working from the slide master on the first thumbnail in the Slides pane.

1. Make sure you're on the **Slide Master** tab. Click inside the top placeholder for the master title style (it reads "Click to edit Master Title style." Title style is not the same as Title slide). All the text will become selected.

2. Click **Fonts** (located in the Edit Theme group), and choose a different font combination (or click Create New Theme Fonts and make your own combination). Do the same with **Colors**.

3. With the heading placeholder still selected, change the text alignment (left-align is **Ctrl+L**; center is **Ctrl+E**; and right-align is **Ctrl+R**.) Or you can click the Home tab, and click the appropriate button in the Paragraph group.

4. Click the **Home** tab, and change font size of heading text to **48** (click the **Font Size** down arrow, and choose **48**).

Format Bullets

You can change the font for the bulleted text using the same method you used for the heading text. You can select and change one line at a time or you can select all the bulleted text by selecting its placeholder, and use one color for all of it. You can also change the bullets. Again, your life would be simpler if you use the pre-set designs.

If you change your bullets, keep them simple. You may want the first level to be a certain color and shape, the second level to look different, and so on.

1. In the Master view, RIGHT-click on the text in the first bullet level, click **Bullets, Bullets and Numbering**. Click to change the bullet shape, color, and to reduce the size to 80 percent of text size (because 100 percent might make the bullet appear too large next to the text).

2. Repeat for each bullet level, keeping everything simple.

3. Click **OK**, then press **Ctrl+S** to save changes you've made to your template.

4. Click the **Home** tab. Increase font size of all bulleted text (starting at 32pt), making the next level slightly smaller than the previous. Select each level of bulleted text, and use the **Increase or Decrease Font Size** button to change the size. Larger text is better for your audience.

   Another way to increase the text size is to click the placeholder surrounding the bulleted text to select it. Then hold down the **Ctrl** key and keep pressing the right bracket] until the text is the size you want.

5. Press **Ctrl+S** to save changes you've made to your template.

6. On the Slide Master tab, click Close Master View.

Line Spacing

You may want to adjust the space between lines or paragraphs on your slides. If you want to make this change to all slides, do it on the master. Otherwise, adjust any slide as needed.

Select the text, RIGHT-click on it, click **Paragraph**. Change the **Spacing** before or after, and change **Line Spacing** as needed. You can change the spacing to something other than the choices of Single, Double, etc., by choosing **Exactly** and typing the desired point size.

📢 *On the Home tab, you can also click the Line Spacing command located in the Paragraph group, and click Line Spacing Options.*

Character Spacing

At some point, you may wish to adjust the spacing between characters in a line of text. For example, you may need to squeeze a few more words on a line.

1. Select the text you need to adjust, and click the **Home** tab.

2. Click the **Character Spacing** button located in the Font group.

3. Choose from the various options that appear (e.g., Very Tight, Tight, etc.).

Create Title Slide

You can design a title slide (your intro slide) using the Title Master layout (the second thumbnail in the Slides pane). It looks different from the master slide in that it has two text placeholders and no bulleted list. You can go with this design or change the background and hide the master objects.

In the section on the header and footer (page 15), you should recall the option, **Don't show on title slide.** With that option ticked, anything you typed as part of the header and footer will not appear on this slide. This gives you greater flexibility in designing a special look and placement for objects on this slide.

Hide Master Background Objects

If you have a slide that needs to look different from the master, you can override some of the customization by formatting the background.

1. In Normal or Slide Sorter view, click the **Home** tab, **New Slide.** For this example, choose the **Title and Content** layout.
2. RIGHT-click on the slide outside of a placeholder, click **Format Background,** tick the **Hide background graphics** box, and click **Close** if no further changes.

Make a Picture Your Slide Background

On some of your slides, you may want a picture to fill up the background instead of the master objects. RIGHT-click on the slide (outside of a placeholder), click **Format Background,** tick **Picture or texture fill.** Next, click the **File** button, find the picture you want to insert, double-click it to insert it, and click **Close.**

If you change your mind later, go back to format the background, and click **Reset Background, Close.**

◀ɳ) *If you want this change to apply to all slides, do this from the master slide.*

Make Your Template the Default

Once you design and save a template, you could make it the default anytime you create a new presentation. If you name your template **blank.potx,** it will become the default design PowerPoint uses when opening new blank presentations.

Replace Master in a Presentation

If you need to replace the master of a presentation with one from a different one, open both presentations.

In the presentation with the master that you want to copy:

1. Go to Slide Master view (click the **View** tab, **Slide Master**). RIGHT-click the top slide in the thumbnail pane on the left, and click **Copy**.

2. Now go to the Slide Master view in the second presentation. RIGHT-click on the top slide in the thumbnail pane on the left, and click **Paste**. (This will create a second master. If you don't need it, RIGHT-click on the top thumbnail slide, and click **Delete Master**.)

📢 *If you created the older presentation without using slide masters, this won't work. You'll have to copy the design elements on the slide and paste onto the master of the newer presentation. Then change your background, footer, etc., on the newer master.*

Create Multiple Masters

If you ever need to have slides in a presentation with different backgrounds, buttons, fonts, etc., you can add multiple masters. However, it's not a good idea to try this until you're comfortable with themes and slide masters as it's too easy to get confused. To create an additional master within a presentation, go to Slide Master view, **Insert Slide Master** (or **Ctrl+M**).

To create an additional master that will have a different theme, click the Master Slide in the thumbnail pane to select it, click **Themes** (in the Edit Theme group), and click to apply desired theme.

If none of this makes sense, you might not be ready for multiple masters.

INSERT NEW SLIDES - SLIDE LAYOUTS

When you click to add a new slide to your presentation (**Home** tab, **New Slide**), the Slide Layout task pane will open. You can choose from the slide layouts such as Title Slide, Title and Content, Section Header, etc.

The layouts will vary based on the template you choose. You can copy and paste layouts from one presentation to another (see page 24).

📢 *You can always make layout changes later by displaying the slide you want to change in Normal view and clicking on another layout (on the **Home** tab, click **Layout** in the Slides group.*

You'll add slides to your presentation using slide layouts. Layouts consist of pre-formatted slides, whether you want a slide with bullets and text, a heading and a graph, a heading and a movie, and so on.

1. Click the **Office** button, **New.** Create a new presentation using either a template you created or from Installed Templates.

2. Double-click the one you want to use. A new title slide will appear. Come back to it later after you've added some slides.

3. On the **Home** tab, click the **New Slide** down arrow, click through the various combinations, and choose a layout for your next slide (for now, choose one with bullets, **Title and Content**).

Change the Current Layout

You can change the layout of a slide on the **Home** tab by clicking the **Layout** drop-down box in the Slides group.

Create a Custom Layout

If you don't find a slide layout that fits your needs, you can create one.

1. From Slide Master view, look for the **Blank Layout** in the list of thumbnails below your slide master, and double-click it to use it. You can click anything in the layout, and **Delete** what you don't need.

2. Add a placeholder and move it (in the Master Layout group, click **Insert Placeholder,** and choose one that fits your needs). Click a location and drag to draw the placeholder (you can resize the placeholder by dragging one of its corners). Use your gridlines to line everything up for a more professional layout (information on aligning objects begins on page 36).

3. Rename your layout. RIGHT-click on the **Blank Layout** thumbnail, and click **Rename**. Give it a sensible name to make it recognizable later.

4. Save your layout as a template (see page 12 for information on creating a template). This new layout will appear with your others when you click the Home tab, Layout in Normal view.

Add Text to Slides

In Normal view, to add text to the title placeholder, just start typing. To add bulleted text, click the text next to the bullet and type. As you add more bulleted text, press **Tab** and **Shift+Tab** to align bullets. You can also click the **Decrease Indent** and **Increase Indent** commands in the Paragraph group.

Eliminate Hanging Indent

When you create a bulleted list, the text will line up in a blocked style away from the bullet. If you decide not to use a bullet and click to turn it off (or click in front of text and Backspace), you'll still have that hanging indent. Select the affected text, and use the mouse to drag the **top marker** under the **first line indent marker**.

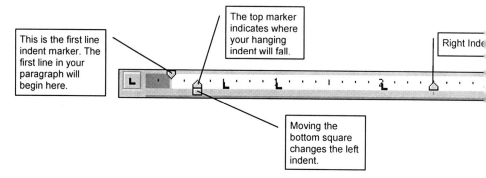

This is the first line indent marker. The first line in your paragraph will begin here.

The top marker indicates where your hanging indent will fall.

Right Inde

Moving the bottom square changes the left indent.

Insert Slides from a Different Presentation

You can add slides from one presentation to another and keep either or both themes. There are two ways to do this: the Copy and Paste or Reuse Slides commands.

Copy and Paste Slides

You can copy a slide in one presentation and paste it into another. From the Slide Pane or from Slide Sorter view, RIGHT-click a slide thumbnail, click **Copy**, go to the second presentation, RIGHT-click where you want the new slide to go, and click **Paste**.

When you paste a slide into a different presentation, the pasted slide will take on the theme of the slide that precedes it. If you want

something different to happen (e.g., you want the pasted slide to keep its theme), click the **Paste Options** button that will appear and tick **Keep Source Formatting** or **Use Destination Theme**. (If your Paste Options button didn't appear, see page 62.)

📢 *You can go to another open presentation by clicking the* **View** *tab,* **Switch Windows.**

Reuse Slides

The second method for inserting slides from one presentation to another is the Reuse Slides command.

1. Create a new presentation or open an old one. Go to Slide Sorter view, and click in the blank space after the slide of which you want the new ones to follow.

2. Click the **Home** tab, **New Slide** drop-down box, **Reuse Slides** (at the bottom). The Reuse Slides task pane will open on the right.

3. Click **Browse**, **Browse File**, and double-click the presentation that has the slides you want. The slides will appear in the task pane.

4. Tick the **Keep source formatting** box (at the bottom of the Reuse Slides task pane) if you want the new slides to remain as is. (If you want the new slides to adapt to the new presentation, leave the box unticked.)

5. Double-click the desired slides (if you want to insert all the slides, RIGHT-click on one of them, and choose Insert All Slides). Close the task pane when done.

📢 *If you're trying to create a new presentation master based on the master of an older presentation, see information on Replace Master in a Presentation on page 21.*

Duplicate a Slide

When you're in Slide Sorter view, click the slide you want to duplicate, **Ctrl+D**. You can click and drag the slide to a new location if needed.

Add Comments to a Slide

If you're reviewing a slide and need to make comments that won't appear during the Show, click the **Review** tab, **New Comment**. If you need to edit a comment later, double-click it. To go from one comment to the next when reviewing your presentation, click the **Previous** and **Next Comment** commands. Click **Delete Comment** when needed.

*You can print the comments separately. When you print your slides (Ctrl+P), the **Print comments and ink markup** box will be ticked by default on the Print dialog box (near the OK button).*

ILLUSTRATIONS – WORKING WITH OBJECTS

◀))) *In PowerPoint, an object is a table, chart, graphic, equation, shape, or other form of information.*

CREATE OR PASTE A TABLE

If you're creating a simple table, click the **Insert** tab, **Table**, click and drag your mouse over the desired number of rows and columns, **OK**. (Or you can click the Table drop-down box, click Draw Table, and click and drag to draw a table with your mouse.) You can also use a slide layout that includes a table (on the Home tab, click New Slide, and choose a content layout such as Two Content).

The table color scheme will match the theme you've chosen for your presentation. You also have access to many table styles when you click the **Design** tab, **More** button (similarly to how you worked with themes, beginning on page 8). If you create your table in Word or use an Excel spreadsheet, you can paste it into PowerPoint, and it'll look the same.

- To add text, click inside the cell and type.
- To make a change to the entire table such as adding color, click the outside border first.

- To make a change to a cell such as turn off a right border, click inside the cell, on the **Design** tab, click **Borders** (in the Table Styles group), and click **Right Border** to turn it off. To change a row or column, select them first.
- To add another row, click the last cell of the table and press **Tab** (or select a row and RIGHT-click).
- To delete a row, select it, and **Ctrl+X** to Cut.
- To change your table's borders, fills, add a shadow, etc., double-click the outside border to activate the **Design** tab. The commands are located in the Table Styles group.
- To resize a table, **Shift+drag** it from the corner. It'll resize proportionately and also increase or decrease font sizes to fit.

INSERT CLIP ART AND PICTURES

To add interest to your slides, you'll want to add photos for a more polished look. I hope not, but sometimes, you might have to settle for clip art.

1. Click on your slide, and click the **Insert** tab. Inside the Illustrations group, click **Clip Art**.

2. The Clip Art Pane will open with various choices.

   - **Search for:** type keywords for the kind of graphic you're looking for.

- **Search in**: If you want to search all categories, click the drop-down box, and tick **Everywhere**. To select specific categories, untick Everywhere (this will make all the boxes blank).

  Now tick the box next to the categories you want to search. Click the **+** sign to display more choices.

- **Results should be**: Choose whether you want photographs, movies, etc., by ticking the appropriate box.

3. In this example, search for "computer" in **All Collections**, and **Photos**. Click **Go**. Once the choices of graphics are displayed, either click and drag one onto your slide, or double-click one to insert it.

If you're online, more clip art, photos, music, etc., are free on the Microsoft® Web site. A link to the site is at the bottom of your Insert Clip Art Pane.

1. Click **Clip art on Office Online** (located at the bottom of the Clip Art Pane), and click the **images** tab on the Microsoft site.

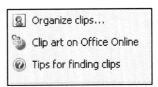

2. Click the desired category, tick **Photo** under **Media types**.

3. Click the desired photo and either click to Download or Add to Basket and keep looking.

📢 My downloaded clips are in this folder: Documents\My Documents\My Pictures\Microsoft Clip Organizer.

Insert a Picture Saved on Your Computer

If you have a picture saved on a disk or on your computer that you want to use, it's easy to insert. Click the **Insert** tab, **Picture** (or click the Insert Picture button on the Quick Access Toolbar).

You'll browse to find it as you normally would, and use one of these options to insert it.

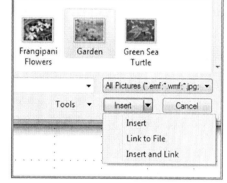

- Double-click the filename to embed the photo into your document, or

- Click the **Insert** drop-down arrow and choose how to insert (**Insert** is a regular insert, and the picture will be embedded in the document, making the file bigger. **Link to File** means you'll insert a link to the picture and when the picture changes in the source file, it'll change in your PowerPoint document. **Insert and Link** means you're embedding the picture into the document as a link back to the source file.)

📢 *If you're going to be presenting on a different computer, make sure any linked files are saved in the same folder (see more information on how to prepare a file to show on a different computer (Package for CD) beginning on page 109).*

Store Objects in the Space Around the Slide

As you start to insert shapes, pictures, etc., you might change your mind about using a particular object. If you think it's a good possibility that you'll use it again, instead of deleting it, drag it off the slide, and save it anywhere in the blue space (PowerPoint's desktop). Your audience will not see it.

Remove White Box

When you insert some objects into PowerPoint, you will probably have to make some adjustments to it. For example, a picture could have a white box around it. This does not look professional on a colored background.

To remove the white box, use the Set Transparent Color command. It samples the color you select and turns it transparent, working best on solid color backgrounds.

1. Click the picture to select it to make the **Format** tab that appears active.

2. In the Adjust group, click **Recolor, Set Transparent Color.**

3. Hold the mouse over the part of the picture you want to make transparent, and click. You will not always have a perfect outcome. Your graphic may become blotchy if it has a lot of color that is the same as the color of the background.

📢 *If you need to delete a background in ClipArt, the transparency tool doesn't work. However, you can ungroup it, convert it to an object, and delete the background.*

Picture Borders

Click your picture to select it. On the **Format** tab that appears, in the Picture Styles group, click one of the options that creates a frame. Change the color of the frame by clicking **Picture Border** and choosing.

Picture Effects

It's easy to add a shadow, reflection, 3-D dimensions to graphics.

1. To add a shadow, reflection, soft edge, or 3-D dimension to a graphic, click it to select it. A **Format** tab will appear, and it'll be active (highlighted). In the Styles group, click **Picture Effects** (or Shape if you're working with a shape), point to **Shadow** (or Soft Edges, Reflection or 3-D, **etc.**), and click an effect. Play with this.

2. To change the position and color of either of these, go back to the effect and click its **Options** at the bottom of the menu. (In this case, you'll point to the **Shadow** effect, and look for **Shadow Options** at the bottom of the resulting dialog box.)

Format Picture as Watermark

If you want a watermark in the background of all your slides, place it on the master. If your watermark is a graphic, insert it as a picture as you normally would. RIGHT-click on it, **Format Picture**. Click to **Recolor**, and under Color Modes, choose the **Washout** option. Use the slider to adjust the color variations.

🔊 *If your watermark is text, use a text box.*

Recolor a Picture

You can recolor a picture directly in PowerPoint. Click or double-

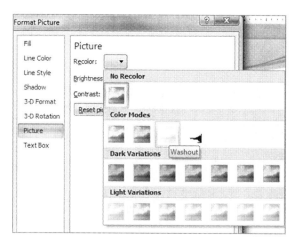

click the picture so the **Format** tab appears. In the Adjust group, click the **Recolor** drop-down list. Hold your mouse over the choices to see what the photo could look like.

Crop a Picture

You can crop away unwanted portions of pictures. Insert a picture and double-click it to select it and make the Format tab active. In the Size group, click the Crop command. You'll notice flat lines and left and right angles have appeared around the edges of the photo.

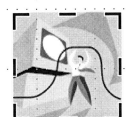

1. Position your mouse over any of them until it turns into what looks like a T turned sideways. Drag in, up, or down to delete the portions of the picture you don't want.

2. If you make a mess, you can reposition the mouse and drag outward to bring the clipped portions back. Or you can click the **Undo** command located on the Quick Access Toolbar (or click the drop-down box and undo as many steps as needed. For example, if you need to Undo the last three actions, highlight them and click. You can also click the **Redo** button to go back and forth. You can't skip around steps).

3. Press **Esc**, or click off the object when finished.

Add Text to a Picture with a Text Box

1. You can add text to a picture using a text box.

2. Insert the picture onto your slide (**Insert** tab, **Picture**), and select it.

3. On the **Home** tab in the Drawing group, click **Text Box**, click on the photo or shape to add the text box, and type desired text.

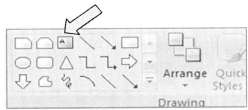

4. To change the font color, size, etc., select the text and RIGHT-click on it. Make desired changes using the shortcut box that will appear.

📢 *A quick way to increase or decrease the size of your text is to select it, then hold down the **Ctrl** key and keep pressing the left bracket key [to decrease, or the right bracket key] to increase.*

Change Text Direction and Wrap Text in Text Box

1. Once you add text to your photo, you may want to change the direction of it (e.g., horizontal).

2. Click the photo to select it, click the **Insert** tab. In the Text group, click **Text Box**, click on the photo to add the text box, and type desired text.

3. Leave the text box selected. In the Paragraph group (on the Home tab), click **Text Direction**, and choose.

📢 *When you first insert a text box, you can drag to draw its width with the mouse.*

Duplicate Formatting with the Format Painter

An often neglected tool is the Format Painter, located on the Home tab inside the Clipboard group. With it, you can copy the formatting of one object and paint it onto another.

1. Draw a new shape, select it, and press **Ctrl+D** to duplicate it. Drag the shapes away from each other.

2. Change the color of one of them, and with it selected, click the **Format Painter** command.

3. Hold the brush over the other shape and click. Watch how it takes on the formatting of the previous shape.

◀ᴵᴵᴵ *To use the Format Painter for several objects, double-click it. When you're finished with it, press Esc.*

CREATE A PHOTO ALBUM

You can create a photo album that consists of a title slide and a collection of graphic images. You can get the images from graphics files or from a scanner or digital camera attached to your computer. Click the **Insert** tab, **Photo Album, New Photo Album**. Instead of trying to explain this command, it's simpler to direct you to a how-to video: www.DigitalBreakthroughs.com/powerpointtutor.htm.

◀ᴵᴵᴵ *Another option for a Photo Album in PowerPoint is from your Installed Template. Click the **Office** button, **New, Installed Templates** (if you're on a company network, instead of clicking Installed Templates, you might see General and Presentation tabs. Click each of these tabs to find the photo album template). Choose **Classic Photo Album** and **Contemporary Photo Album.** To change any photos, RIGHT-click on it, click **Change Picture**, and browse. Double-click the desired graphic to replace the default.*

SHAPES - CREATE, ALIGN, AND COLOR

Create Shapes

Use shapes to create rectangles, squares, straight lines, perfect circles, etc. Click the **Insert** tab, **Shapes**. To draw, click the desired shape, then hold the mouse (which is now a crosshair) over your slide, and click and drag the mouse to draw.

▤   If you click the oval tool (or the rectangle tool), then click on the slide and don't drag, a circle (or square) will appear. To resize it, hold down the **Shift** key as you drag to maintain the shape.

▤ If you need to draw multiple shapes, one after the other, RIGHT-click it, and click **Lock Drawing Mode**. Press **Esc** when done.

▤ If you hold down the **Shift** key as you draw, the rectangle tool will draw a square, the oval tool will draw a circle, and your lines will draw straight.

▤ If you're drawing lines, keep them straight by holding down the **Shift** key.

Change Order of Objects

You'll often want to rearrange how objects are placed on the slide. One may be on top of another, and you'll want it on the bottom or vice versa. If you have multiple objects on top of each other, you can move them by layer.

1. Draw a circle on top of a square. Select the object you want to change the order of.

2. In the Arrange group, click **Send to Back**.

   ▤ **Bring to Front**. Object will come in front of whatever is placed on top of it.

   ▤ **Send to Back**. Object will go behind everything.

   ▤ **Bring Forward**. Object will come in front of objects layer by layer. To see this command, click the drop-down box next to Bring to Front.

   ▤ **Send Backward**. Object will go behind other items layer by layer. To see this command, click the drop-down box next to Send to Back.

Select Several Objects at Once

Anytime you need to select more than one object, use your mouse and drag over them. When you release the mouse, all the objects will be selected. Did you miss one? Hold down the Shift key, and click it. Click anywhere off of the selection to de-select.

Selection and Visibility Pane

A new feature in PowerPoint 2007 is the Selection and Visibility pane. You can use it to select objects, change the order, etc. The Selection and Visibility pane can also be used to select multiple objects. To use this command, double-click any object on a slide so the **Format** tab becomes active. In the Arrange group, click **Selection Pane**.

All objects on a slide will appear in the Selection and Visibility pane, including shapes, pictures, movies and sound, WordArt, text boxes, and placeholders (if you see an object on the slide and it's not in the Selection pane, it's either on one of the master slides or is the actual background of the slide).

You can do the following inside the Selection pane:

- Select multiple objects by holding down the **Ctrl** key and clicking them. To select everything, click at least one item to select it, then press **Ctrl+A**.

- **Re-order** the layering of objects by clicking the buttons at the bottom of the pane. (Later, you'll learn how to move objects in front of or behind another (starting on page 36). Using the re-order command can be used as an easier way to do this.)

- Make an object invisible by clicking the **Eye icon** on the right side of the list (if you don't see this icon, hold your mouse over the right-edge of the pane, and drag it left to widen it). Later, you'll discover that the ability to hide objects will make it easier to edit your custom animations and images.

▤ Rename objects to make them more recognizable at a glance (e.g., instead of Picture 41, I renamed it CNN). To change the name, I double-clicked Picture 41, then single-clicked. Once the name became highlighted with a box around it, I typed the new name. Click anywhere off of it when done.

When the Selection and Visibility Pane is not in use, click the **X** to close it.

Align Objects

It's important to align objects with precision on a page for a more professional look. There are several ways to do this. You can align objects with each other or in relation to the entire slide. You can also arrange (or distribute) objects so they are equal distances from each other, either vertically or horizontally, or in relation to the entire slide.

Align Using the Grid

A grid is an invisible matrix used to automatically align objects in relation to the slide (you can choose to view it). Grids are not visible in a presentation, and they do not print. To see them as you create your slides, you'll have to turn them on.

If you have Grid on as you draw or move objects, their corners will automatically align at the nearest intersection of the grid. This is called snap to grid. You'll want to leave snap to grid on and only turn it off as needed. To turn the Grid on or off:

1. Click the **Home** tab. In the Drawing group, click **Arrange**, point to **Align**, click **Grid Settings** to open the Grid and Guides dialog box.

2. Tick **Snap objects to grid** if it's blank. To see the grid on the screen, tick **Display grid on screen** if it's blank.

Once the grid is turned on, when you need to nudge or crop an object and you're having a hard time getting what you want, temporarily turn off the snap by holding down the **Alt** key as you drag the object.

For example, I was trying to crop a picture, and I needed to get very close to the edge. Snap to grid was preventing it because the spacing of the grid (called a grid unit) was too wide (you'll see this in the Grid and Guides dialog box). I could have changed the spacing to put the grids closer together, but I turned it off temporarily by holding down the Alt key as I dragged. That gave me more control over my mouse actions.

Align Using Guides

A guide is another visual cue you can use to align objects using your mouse (or the keyboard arrow keys). They are turned on by default and are the dotted vertical and horizontal lines you see in Normal view (they don't print). To align objects using a guide, move them to rest up against it.

You can display guides if they're not visible. Click the **Home** tab. In the Drawing group, click **Arrange**, point to **Align**, click **Grid Settings**, tick **Display drawing guides on screen**. Or **Alt+F9** to turn them on and off.

Move or Add More Guides

You can move guides around by holding the mouse over one and dragging it to different locations. You can add as many additional guides as you need.

1. Hold your mouse over one of the guides (make sure you're outside of any placeholders).

2. With your mouse directly over a guide, hold down the **Ctrl key** as you click and drag (you should see some measurements as you drag). You can continue to add as many as you need.

Remove Guides

To remove a guide, click it and drag it off the edge of your slide. To hide all of them at once, hold down **Alt** and press **F9** (**Alt+F9**). Repeat to bring them back.

Measure Distance Between Objects

To get the precise measurement of the distance between objects, hold down the Shift key as you drag a guide between them.

Align or Distribute Command

The best way to align objects is by using commands in the Drawing group.

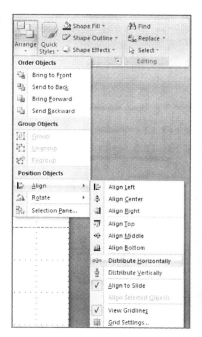

1. Draw two or more shapes, and place them in a line next to each other. Select the shapes (hold down the **Shift** key as you select each object, or drag your mouse around the objects you want to select).

2. With all objects selected, click the **Home** tab. In the Drawing group, click **Arrange**, point to **Align**, click **Distribute Horizontally.**

Move the objects around, and try the various options. For example, to align the object evenly on the bottom or top, choose **Align Bottom** or **Align Top.**

Group and Ungroup Objects

You can group multiple objects on a slide and make them behave as one. On the other hand, when objects have been computer-drawn (such as clip art), you can ungroup the pieces and move one at a time. You can always regroup them as needed.

Ungroup an Object and Edit

1. In Normal view, insert clip art onto your slide by clicking the **Insert** tab. Browse to find clip art, and drag it onto your slide as explained previously (refer back to the information on inserting pictures beginning on page 28, if you need to).

2. RIGHT-click the graphic, point to Group, click Ungroup. Click Yes to convert the imported object to a Microsoft Office drawing. RIGHT-click again to ungroup.

3. Continue to ungroup your object until it becomes covered in selection boxes. This assures that all the pieces that went into creating this graphic are selected.

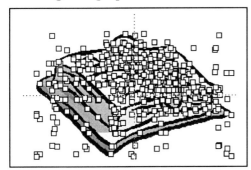

4. Click anywhere off the object to clear selection boxes.

5. RIGHT-click on the pieces to see if they can be ungrouped even more (unless you see that what you need is separated enough).

*The keyboard shortcut for Group is **Ctrl+G**. Ungroup is **Ctrl+Shift+G**.*

Regroup an Object

If you ungrouped an object and didn't add any additional drawing objects to it, you can Regroup it quickly because PowerPoint remembers. RIGHT-click on any portion of the previously ungrouped object, point to **Group**, and click **Regroup**.

If, on the other hand, you have ungrouped an object and added something to it, you'll need to Group it. Use your mouse to draw a marquee around all the objects you want to group. Once everything is selected (selection boxes will appear on selected objects. If you missed something, hold down the Shift key and click it), RIGHT-click it, point to **Group**, click **Group** (not Regroup).

Recolor an Object

Once you have an object ungrouped, you'll be able to pull any pieces apart and use it, recolor it, etc., as you would a shape created inside PowerPoint (select the piece you want to recolor, and use Shape Fills on the Format tab).

Rotate Objects

You can rotate objects by varying degrees.

1. Draw a shape and click it to select it. Hold your mouse pointer over the green circle at the top of the graphic until the mouse pointer turns into a rotate tool.
2. Drag the mouse in different directions to rotate the graphic.

If you add text to a shape, the text will rotate along with it.

Duplicate and Flip Objects

1. In Normal view, continue working with the clip art.
2. Duplicate the graphic by selecting it and pressing **Ctrl+D**.
3. Drag the duplicate object to a new location on the slide.

4. Keep the graphic you want to flip selected. Click the **Rotate** command in the Arrange group, and choose.

Add Text to Your Shapes

You can easily add text inside a shape.

1. Click the shape and start typing. Click anywhere off the shape when finished.

2. Edit the text by clicking inside the shape and changing text as you normally would (or right-click on the shape and click **Edit Text**).

Change Alignment of Text Inside Shapes

To change how text appears in a text box, RIGHT-click on the text box, and click **Format Shape** (make sure you have the text box selected and not the shape). In the resulting dialog box, click **Text Box**. You'll be able to:

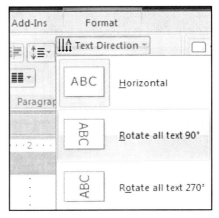

- Change the text layout (alignment inside and the text direction).

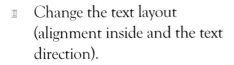

- Tick Autofit (so the text box doesn't automatically resize to fit the text).

- Change the internal margins so text fits closer or farther away from the edge.

- Choose to wrap text inside the shape.

Shape Background

Use Picture as Shape Background

You can add a picture to the background of a shape. Draw any shape and double-click it so the **Format** tab appears. In the Shape Styles group, click **Shape Fill, Picture or texture fill,** find the desired picture, and double-click it to insert inside the shape. If you change your mind, repeat the steps.

If you insert a picture into your presentation that you want to animate, put it inside a shape and apply the animation to that instead of to the picture on its own. This way, if you decide to change the picture, you won't have to redo the animation. You'll learn more about animation in a subsequent lesson.

Add Slide Background to Shape

If you ever want the slide background to also serve as the background of a shape, RIGHT-click the shape (make sure it's selected), click **Format Shape, Fill,** and tick **Slide background fill, Close**.

If you change your mind later, repeat the steps and choose Solid Fill.

Create Default Shape

You can make changes to a shape and make that the default for the current presentation. Draw a shape and make changes to it (fill, border, shadow, etc.). RIGHT-click on it, and click **Set as Default Shape**.

This new default will only work in the current presentation.

Change to a Different Shape

After you draw a shape, you can change it to a different one and keep your formatting intact. Double-click the shape you want to change to activate the **Format** tab. On the Format tab, you'll see the Insert Shapes group. Click **Edit Shape**, point to **Change Shape**, and click the desired shape.

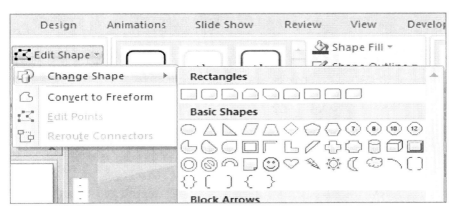

📢 *Don't confuse the Insert tab/Shapes command with the Insert Shapes group located on the Format tab.*

Reshape a Shape

Certain shapes can be reshaped and made to look completely different from what you started with. Under **Basic Shapes**, draw the **Sun** shape. The yellow diamond that appears is the reshape tool (look closely). Hold your mouse over it and click and drag to change the shape.

You can reshape the sun by dragging the yellow diamond.

Edit a Shape with Freeform

You may need to change a shape beyond using the reshape tool. In this example, you have a block arrow that you want to change the base and indent it so you can something such as text there.

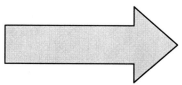

1. Click the shape to select it and display the **Format** tab (if the Format tab isn't active, double-click the shape). In the Insert Shapes group, click **Edit Shape, Convert to Freeform**.

2. Click **Edit Shape** again, but this time click **Edit Points**. You should notice the black points at every intersection of the graphic.

3. Hold your mouse over midway the base of the arrow, and you'll notice a new four-pointed edit point. Click and drag inward as shown.

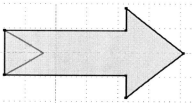

4. Release the mouse, and the shape will now look like this.

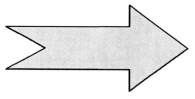

5. Click anywhere on an outside border and reshape as desired. (Yes, I know there is an arrow like this in Shapes, but humor me and do this anyway.)

Recolor Shapes – Inside and the Border

1. Click one of your shapes. A **Format** tab will appear and it'll be active (highlighted). In the Shape Styles group, click **Shape Fill**, and choose a color.

2. Change the border color by clicking **Shape Outline** and choosing a color. Then click **Shape Outline** again, and change the weight (thickness) of the border.

You can also make multiple changes to a shape by RIGHT-clicking it and choosing **Format Shape**.

Make a Shape Transparent

Anytime you want an object to be transparent, follow the instructions for recoloring shapes, and choose **No Fill, No Line**.

Create a Slide Border Using a Shape

You can frame a slide. Draw the rectangle shape over the entire slide. With the shape selected, click the **Format** tab. Change the **Shape Fill** to **No Fill**. Then change the color and weight (thickness) of the **Shape Outline** as desired. (More elaborate borders can be found in Clip Art (instructions on inserting clip art start on page 28). Search for "borders." After you insert the one you want, you can rotate or flip it to make it look the way you want.)

Save a Shape as a Picture

You can create a shape or object in PowerPoint and save it as a picture. RIGHT-click on the shape, and click **Save as Picture** (it's aggravating, but you'll often see this Move Here Copy Here shortcut when you right-click. Move the mouse to a different location on the graphic and RIGHT-click again). I usually save all graphics as JPEGs.

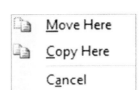

ACTION BUTTONS

You can insert Action Buttons onto a slide with hyperlinks assigned to them. The hyperlinks help you navigate to various slides, custom shows, and other files and Web pages during the slide show. The buttons include actions such as Home, Back, etc. These buttons will mostly likely go on your master slide in order to appear on all slides.

1. Click the **View** tab, **Slide Master**, **Insert** tab, **Shapes**, scroll down to the bottom for **Action Buttons.**

2. Click the button for **Home**, hold down the left mouse button and drag to create a button. Release the mouse when done.

3. The Action Settings dialog box appears once you release the mouse. The **Hyperlink to First Slide** option (home page) is already selected (because you chose the Home button), so click **OK** (or you can click the **Mouse Over** tab and use this option).

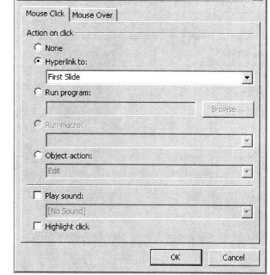

4. Recolor the button or resize it when you're back on the slide master (RIGHT-click on it, **Format Shape**). Launch the show (**F5**) to see how everything works.

Later, if you want to make a change, go back to the slide master RIGHT-click on the button, Edit Hyperlink.

The Home Action Button was placed on the master slide so it would appear on every slide automatically.

Create Your Own Action Button

You can add various actions to a button (or use any graphic as described later).

1. Repeat the previous steps but instead of choosing Home, draw the **Blank** button. The None option is already ticked, so choose which slide, file, URL, etc., you want to link to (scroll down so you see all the options).

2. Scroll down, and click **Other File**. Browse to find a file on your computer to link the button to, double-click it, click **OK**.

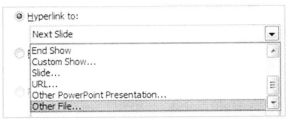

To add text to your button, simply start typing while the button is selected. You can format the text and recolor the button as you normally would.

Use a Graphic as Your Action Button

If you have a graphic you want to use as an Action Button, you can. Place it on the master slide if you want it to appear on all slides, or wherever it's needed. Create a hyperlink to the desired Web page, file, etc. See more information on creating hyperlinks on page 82.

INSERT SMARTART

In PowerPoint 2007, you can create designer-quality illustrations, called SmartArt, as easily as you can insert a square shape. The type of SmartArt you choose will depend on the purpose of the graphic.

Regardless of the graphic you choose, it should be clear and easy to follow. This is best achieved by using shorter amounts of text.

1. Click the **Insert** tab, **SmartArt** (located in the Illustrations group). You'll be prompted to choose a type of SmartArt graphic such as **List** or **Hierarchy.** A more detailed description of each graphic's purpose appears as you click it.

Graphic Type	Purpose of Graphic
List	Show non-sequential information.
Process	Show steps in a process or timeline.
Cycle	Show a continual process.
Hierarchy	Show a decision tree.
Hierarchy	Create an organization chart.
Relationship	Illustrate connections.
Matrix	Show how parts relate to a whole.
Pyramid	Show proportional relationships with the largest component on the top or bottom.

2. Double-click the desired graphic to place it on your slide. You can always change it later.

3. Placeholder text such as [Text] will appear (the border around the graphic and the placeholder text don't print or show during your slide show).

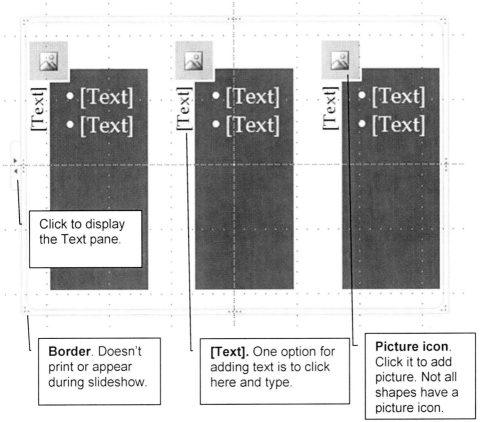

Click to display the Text pane.

Border. Doesn't print or appear during slideshow.

[Text]. One option for adding text is to click here and type.

Picture icon. Click it to add picture. Not all shapes have a picture icon.

4. Add text to the graphic by doing one of the following.

   ▤ Click [**Text**] in the Text pane, and then type (best way).

   ▤ Click and type directly inside the graphic.

   ▤ Copy text from another location or program, click [**Text**] in the Text pane, and paste.

◀)) *When you're using SmartArt, it's important to get your words right first, then fine-tune your graphic.*

SmartArt's Text Pane

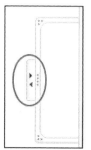 The Text pane appears when you click the SmartArt graphic. If you don't see it, click the tab as shown. You should use the Text pane to add and manage your text that will appear in each graphic. Consequently, you'll be able to concentrate more on the verbiage and worry about how the graphic will look later.

Adding Bulleted Text (or Shapes)

When you create the SmartArt, the number of shapes is determined by how many first-level bullets or paragraphs you have. As you add and edit your content in the Text Pane, your SmartArt graphic is automatically updated, adding or deleting shapes as needed. You can also add a shape by RIGHT-clicking on one of the shapes, **Add Shape**.

To add or edit text in the Text Pane, click [**Text**] and start typing. To add another bullet under the first one, press **Enter**. You can use your keyboard down arrow key to go to the next bullet that's already there. You can promote or demote the text by pressing **Tab** to promote and **Shift+Tab** to demote.

📢 *The Promote and Demote commands are also located on the Design tab inside the Create Graphic group.*

Deleting Bulleted Text (or Shapes)

You can select any shape you need to delete, and press **Delete**. The SmartArt will adjust itself automatically. To delete text using the Text Pane, move your cursor at the end of the bulleted text that's before the text that's to be deleted, and press **Delete**.

For example, you have three shapes with text: Flowers, Trees, Nature. You decide to remove the Nature shape. You'll place your cursor inside the Text pane after the word Trees, and press **Delete**.

- Flowers

- Trees

- Nature

Change SmartArt Layout and Styles

After you get the text the way you want it, you might want to change the layout. Click the border of the SmartArt to select it. A special **Design** tab will appear with options specific to SmartArt (these are SmartArt Tools). In the Layouts group, click the **More** button, **More Layouts**, click desired layout (you can always change again later).

With the graphic still selected, move over to the SmartArt Styles group (click the **More** button for additional options).

Customize the SmartArt Graphic

You can customize the SmartArt graphic by adding, removing, resizing, or moving shapes. For more help with the following topics, refer to a demo on my Website: www.DigitalBreakthroughs.com/powerpointtutor.htm.

Recolor SmartArt

Most of the time, you'll use the colors that come with the theme you've chosen or created for your presentation. However, you can recolor a SmartArt graphic whenever needed. Click the border around it so the entire graphic is selected. Click the **Design** tab, **Change Colors**, choose a new color scheme.

You can also change an individual shape by RIGHT-clicking on it, **Format Shape**, and change the **Fill Color**, **Line Color**, etc.

📢 *If you want only the text in your text box to appear, set the text box to have no background color (No Fill) and no border (No Line).*

Add a Picture to SmartArt

On some SmartArt, you'll see a picture icon. To replace the icon, click it, choose a picture, and double-click it to place on the slide.

Add a Shape to SmartArt

When you're not working inside the Text pane, you can quickly add

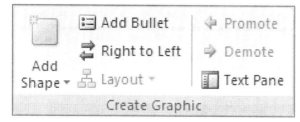

a shape to your graphic by RIGHT-clicking on any shape, **Add Shape**. Or you can click the **Design** tab, then click the shape that's closest to where you want to add one. In the Create Graphic group, click the **Add Shape button**. If you need to choose where the new shape will land, click the Add Shape drop-down box (instead of clicking the button), and choose the desired location.

Use Text Box with SmartArt

When you need text to appear close to or on top of your SmartArt graphic, use a text box. Click the **Insert** tab, **Text Box**. Click on your slide where you want the text box to appear, and type. To add a fill color or border, RIGHT-click on the border of the text box, **Format Shape**.

Delete a Shape from SmartArt Graphic

To delete a shape from your SmartArt graphic, click the shape you want to delete, **Delete** key. (If a shape such as an arrow on your SmartArt won't delete, RIGHT-click on it, click Format Shape, and change to No Fill, No Line Color.)

Change or Reset a Shape in SmartArt

You can easily change one or more shapes in a SmartArt graphic. Select the shape or shapes you want to change, RIGHT-click on the selection, click **Change Shape**, click the new shape. To start over, either click **Undo** (or select the graphic, click Reset Graphic).

Resize SmartArt Graphic or Shapes

To resize your entire graphic, click the border and drag the sizing handles in or out. To resize a shape within the graphic, click it to select it, and resize it by dragging one of the resizing handles that appear (to keep the graphic in proportion, only drag from a corner). Or click the Format tab, Larger or Smaller (in the Shapes group).

Create an Organization Chart

To create an organization chart, click the **Insert** tab, **SmartArt**, **Hierarchy**, and double-click the **Organization Chart**. RIGHT-click on the boxes you want to add to, and click **Add Shape**, and make your choices. If you need to delete a shape, click it to select it, and press **Delete**.

📢 *If you choose any other style other than Organization Chart, the Add Assistant command will not be available.*

Convert Slide Text to SmartArt

If you already have text on a slide such as a bulleted list, you can convert it to SmartArt. Click the placeholder surrounding the text you want to change, and click the **Home** tab. In the Paragraphs group, click **Convert to SmartArt Graphic**, click desired layout, and make changes as previously explained. (This command only works in PowerPoint.)

Reuse a SmartArt Graphic

To save time, you can copy and paste a SmartArt graphic from one presentation to another (and also to another Office document). If you used an Office theme, your graphic will change to match it.

Animate SmartArt

You can animate your SmartArt graphic and have each unit appear at the same time, one at a time, etc. Click the border of the SmartArt, and click the **Animations** tab. In the Animations group, click the **Animate** drop-down box, and hover your mouse over the command to see how it displays. Click the one you want to use.

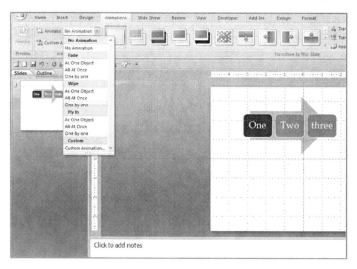

You'll also be able to apply custom animation to your SmartArt (page 69). While you're here, decide how you want to Advance Slide (either On Mouse Click or Automatically After desired time.)

CREATE AND INSERT CHARTS

You can use the data in a spreadsheet and create all sorts of picture representations of it by creating charts. You can originate a chart directly in PowerPoint, but you'll end up working in Excel. When you make changes to the Excel data, the chart updates dynamically.

The following discussion applies if you also have Excel 2007 installed on your computer. If you don't, the old Microsoft Graph will appear (some of the following instructions will not apply).

Spreadsheet Layout for Charts

To understand how charting works, you have to first understand the layout of the data in the table and how it translates to the chart. Selecting the right data in the table is crucial to creating a chart that will make sense.

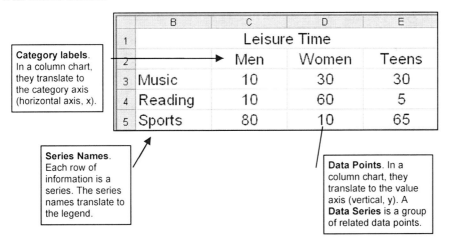

Category labels. In a column chart, they translate to the category axis (horizontal axis, x).

Series Names. Each row of information is a series. The series names translate to the legend.

Data Points. In a column chart, they translate to the value axis (vertical, y). A Data Series is a group of related data points.

Chart Terms

Most charts have two axes, the category axis and the value axis. The category axis displays text labels such as months, cities, sales representatives, etc. The value axis always displays numerical data, such as currency amounts, percents, etc. Depending on the type of chart, the particular axis could be horizontal (X axis) or vertical (Y axis), depending on which set of data is the focus of the chart.

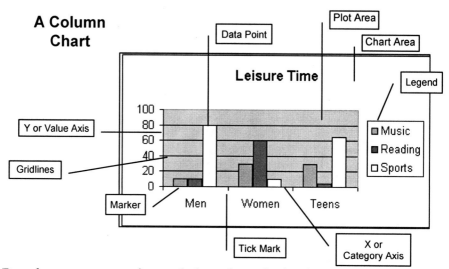

Bar charts compare data side-by-side with the focus on the value axis (horizontal axis). Column charts also compare data side-by-side, but with the focus on the category axis (horizontal axis). The column chart is the default chart in PowerPoint, so start with it first to determine if it'll give you what you need. Later, you'll create a default template.

- **Axis.** Forms the boundaries of the chart and contains the scale for plotting data.

- **Data Point.** A single piece of data, such as the number of men who listened to music for leisure.

- **Data Series.** A collection of data points, such as all the people who enjoyed reading as a leisure activity. Each data series has a unique color or pattern (pie charts have only one data series).

- **Chart Area.** All the area that surrounds the chart.

- **Gridlines.** Lines you add to make it easier to view data.

- **Legend.** A guide outside the chart that explains the symbols, patterns, or colors used to distinguish the different data series.

- ▤ **Marker.** An object that represents a data point, such as bars, pies, and so on.

- ▤ **Plot Area.** The shaded area surrounding all the plotted area.

- ▤ **Tick Mark.** A division mark along the Category and Value axis.

📢) *When you right- or left-click on a chart, a light-blue frame surrounds it. This lets you know that the chart is selected.*

Data Series

The data series, a collection of associated data, can be plotted by row or by column. In this example, the data series is **all** the people who enjoyed listening to music (or reading or sports) for leisure. This information translates to the category axis.

	B	C	D	E
1		Leisure Time		
2		Men	Women	Teens
3	Music	10	30	30
4	Reading	10	60	5
5	Sports	80	10	65

Chart Data by Row

Charting data by row plots it based on the series names (row titles). The series names Music, Reading, and Sports form the legend.

Chart Data by Column

On the other hand, charting by column plots data based on the category labels (column titles). The category labels in the table below are Men, Women, and Teens, and form the legend.

📢) *If you're charting by row and want to switch to charting by column, you can change. RIGHT-click anywhere on the chart, click **Select Data, Switch Row/Column** button. If you don't like the results, click the Undo button.*

Create a Chart from Inside PowerPoint

You can either create a new chart directly in PowerPoint, or create it in Excel and paste it into PowerPoint.

To create it inside PowerPoint, create a new slide and click the **Insert** tab, **Chart**, choose the chart style you need, and double-click it to insert onto your slide.

An Excel worksheet will appear along with your chart. All of your data manipulation will be done in Excel. Maximize the Excel window, and replace the default data with your own. As you add more rows and columns, the data range will adjust (or you can resize the data range by dragging the blue corner).

When you've finished adding your data, you can close the Excel worksheet. It's saved with the PowerPoint file automatically.

Your Excel spreadsheet should not have any blank cells within the data when used for charting.

Reopen a Worksheet

To open the worksheet in PowerPoint later, RIGHT-click anywhere on the chart, and click **Edit Data**. Your worksheet will open ready for editing. As you make changes to it, the chart in PowerPoint will change also.

Change Chart Type

The initial chart type you chose might not fit your needs. To change it, RIGHT-click anywhere on the chart, and in the Type group, click **Change Chart Type**.

When you right- or left-click on a chart, a light-blue frame surrounds it. This lets you know the chart is selected.

Formatting Your Chart

You have lots of options for adding punch to your chart. The best way to get acquainted with these design elements is to spend some time playing with them.

- RIGHT-click on the portion of the chart you want to change. For example, to change the background of the chart area, RIGHT-click anywhere on it, and click **Format Chart Area**.

- Or click the **Layout** tab, and choose what you want to select from the Current Selection group.

- Select the chart and click the **Layout** tab for other options such as adding a Chart Title.

Widen the Bars on a Chart

If you create a bar chart and the bars look too narrow, you can widen them. Insert a bar chart, click one of the bars to select the entire data series. RIGHT-click on one of the selected bars, and click **Format Data Series**. Ensure that **Series Options** is active, and reduce the **Gap Width**.

Create a Chart Starting from Excel

If you already have data in Excel (or you're starting with a new worksheet) and need a chart, select the data you want charted, and press **F11**. A new worksheet will be added to your Excel workbook that contains the chart. On the other hand, if you want to keep the chart on the same worksheet as the data, select the data you want to chart, and press **Alt+F1**.

You'll format and design your chart in Excel as explained previously.

After you've finished designing the chart, insert it into PowerPoint as a link back to Excel. This way, anytime you change the data in Excel, the PowerPoint chart changes also.

1. Save the Excel file before attempting to insert the chart into a presentation.

2. Open the Excel file, and select the chart (click on it so the border appears and click the border), and press **Ctrl+C** to copy it to the Clipboard (or RIGHT-click on the border and click Copy).

3. Open your PowerPoint presentation, and click where you want to paste your chart. Click the **Paste down arrow** (located in the Clipboard group), **Paste Special, Paste Link**.

📢 *Later, when you make changes in Excel, check your presentation to ensure the changes happened in PowerPoint. You may have to RIGHT-click the chart, and click **Update Link**.*

Paste Options Button

Continuing from the previous lesson, another way to paste an Excel chart into PowerPoint is with the Paste Options button. When you use the paste keyboard shortcut (**Ctrl+V**), the Paste Options button will appear (if not, turn it on. Click the Office button, Advanced, tick Show Paste Options buttons). Paste the chart again.

The following options are available.

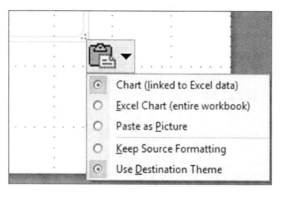

▤ **Chart (Linked to Excel Data)**. The chart updates when the data is changed in Excel. This is probably what you'll want to do most of the time.

▤ **Excel Chart (entire workbook)**. Your data is copied over to PowerPoint.

▤ **Paste as Picture**. An image of the chart is copied but cannot be changed further. If you're sending your presentation to someone, you may want to use this if you have formulas in your Excel spreadsheet that need to be protected.

The following options relate to how the chart looks after it's pasted:

- Keep Source Formatting. Use this if you want the chart to keep its design as is.

- Use Destination Theme. Use this if you want the chart to take on the look of the presentation you're pasting it into (this will work if you're using one of PowerPoint's built-in themes).

Update Your Excel Data and Chart

If you need to change data in an existing cell, click inside and type the new information as you normally would. If you need to add additional columns or rows, you'll have to expand the range by dragging the blue line that borders the data. (If you don't see the blue line, click the chart border.) Drag from one of the corners.

When you've finished updating the information, do one of the following:

- If the chart is linked (you created it in Excel), save the worksheet as you normally would.

- If the chart is embedded (you created it inside PowerPoint), close the worksheet. PowerPoint saves the embedded chart automatically. The worksheet is saved along with the presentation.

Default Chart Style

If you're always creating the same style of chart (e.g., Scatter), store it as the default. Create a chart in PowerPoint or Excel as you normally would. Once the chart is created, select it by clicking near its edge to display the border. RIGHT-click the border, click **Change Chart Type, Set as Default Chart, OK**.

Later, when you create a new chart, click the **Insert** tab, **Chart, OK.** Your default style chart will be created.

Even better, if you want to create a default chart with special colors, etc., you'll have to save it as a template. Then you can save that template as the default.

Create a Chart Template and Reuse Later

You can design a chart, save it as a template, reuse it, or send it to

someone. Design your chart as you normally would. From Design mode (double-click the outside border to ensure you're in Design mode), click the **Save As Template** button located in the Type group. Give the template a descriptive name. Everything will be saved as part of the template except any data.

To use your template later, you must first open the chart's data source in Excel 2007 (double-click the chart). With the data source open, click the **Insert** tab, **Chart** button, **Templates**, double-click the desired template, **OK.**

🔊 *Do not try to apply a chart template to an existing chart. You could lose all your data.*

Your chart template will not follow the theme of your presentation. If you use different color schemes and a lot of charts, you'll want to create a chart template to go with each color scheme.

🔊 *To prevent an error, you must first open the chart's data source in Excel 2007, and then apply the custom chart template. Otherwise, PowerPoint could shut down.*

Save a Chart Template as the Default

If you usually use the same chart template, save it as the default. Repeat the steps in the previous lesson, but after you click the Templates folder, click the template you want to use as the default, and click the **Set as Default Chart** button.

Create a Chart Based on Default Template

Now that you've established a default chart template, a quick way to create future charts is to select the data you want charted and press **F11**. A new worksheet will be added to your Excel workbook and contain the chart.

On the other hand, if you want to create a chart based on the default, but keep it on the same worksheet as the data, select the data you want to chart, and press **Alt+F1**. Either way, you'll be able to resize the chart or copy and paste it somewhere else.

Animate a Chart

During your presentation, you may want the chart elements to appear one series at a time, as one object, etc. It's easy to apply animation to your chart.

Animating your chart works the same as you learned for animating SmartArt (beginning on page 56). Select the chart (the faded blue box will appear to let you know it's selected), click the **Animations** tab, choose the type of animation you want.

Chart Custom Animation

You can tweak the animation in the previous lesson using Custom Animation. For example, you might not want the entire chart to animate, the bars to Wipe Down instead of Up, you want to time the appearance of each bar instead of using the mouse to advance, etc. All of this and more can be done using custom animation.

1. Select the chart, and click **Custom Animation** on the **Animations** tab. The Custom Animation pane will open (if Add Effect is grayed out, you didn't select the chart).

2. Click the **Add Effect** button, point to **Entrance**, and click the **Blinds** animation (or any you desire).

3. Double-click the chart animation now listed in the task pane (or click the drop-down box).

4. In the dialog box that opens, click the **Chart Animation** tab. Choose the chart element you want to animate. For this example, choose **By Series**, and untick the box next to **Start animation by drawing the chart background**.

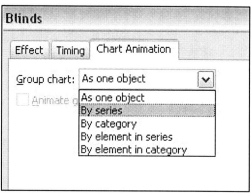

5. Add other animation effects as you've learned earlier, and click OK.

6. Click off the chart to deselect it.

WordArt

WordArt, a tool that gives shapes to words, was probably one of the first fun things you did in PowerPoint. By itself, WordArt can look downright ugly. I never used it until I discovered all the ways I could dress it up. You can add background pictures, shadows, 3-D effects, etc., to it just as you would other objects.

1. Click the **Insert** tab. In the Text group, click **WordArt**. The WordArt Gallery will open. Click any desired style.

2. Type your text to replace "Your Text Here" while the text box is selected. You can change the text later if needed by selecting it.

3. Click to change the fill colors, add a picture inside the text, change the borders, or change the text effects in the WordArt Styles group. Click through each of these for various options.

4. Change the font by selecting the text and RIGHT-clicking on it. Click **Font** and make desired changes. Or you can RIGHT-click anywhere on the border of the text box and make your changes in the shortcut box that appears.

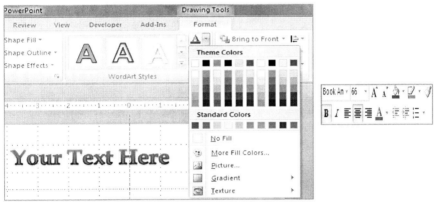

Add a Picture to Background of WordArt

You can add a picture to the background of WordArt just as you can to a shape in the previous lesson. With the WordArt text selected, click the **Text Fill** command that's located in the WordArt Styles group (not Shape Fill), click **Picture**, choose the picture, and double-click it to insert inside your WordArt.

Add Picture to WordArt

SLIDE TRANSITIONS

You can enhance your presentation by changing how your slides appear as you click from one to the next (transition). For a more professional presentation, keep the different transitions to a minimum. However, you could use a different transition for a slide that's introducing a new topic.

Transitions can also be used as a subtle way to psychologically convey your message. The following is a list of how different transitions can be used to do this.

- Progression, positive, going forward: Choose a transition that moves UP or RIGHT.

- Regression, negative, moving backward: Choose a transition that moves DOWN or LEFT.

- The opening of a window of opportunity: Choose an OUT transition.

- Starting over, out with the old and in with the new: Choose an IN transition.

To work with transitions, go to Slide Sorter view (click the **View** tab, **Slide Sorter,** or click it on the Slide Changer).

1. Select a slide, and click the **Animations** tab. In the Transition to This Slide group, click the different transitions, and change **Transition Speed** to Medium.

2. Change how the slide will advance. For example, untick **On mouse click,** and tick to advance **Automatically After** 3 seconds (00:03). Click Apply To All when needed on all slides.

3. Click the Slide Show icon on the Slide Changer to launch the show from the current slide (or Shift+F5).

ANIMATION

You can add motion to text, pictures, and other elements on your slides and control how and when the effects happen. These effects

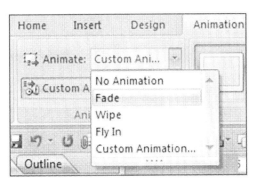

will draw your audience's attention to certain points and add pizzazz to your presentation. Don't overdo it.

You can choose to animate an object using one of the built-in animations (click the object to select it, **Animations** tab, the **Animate** drop-down box,

and choose Fade, Wipe, or Fly-In). To go beyond that, you'll have to use custom animation.

CUSTOM ANIMATION

In order to fully understand how custom animation works for the different types of objects you'll insert into your presentation, you're going to have to spend some time playing around in the dialog box, clicking your way through the different tabs and choices.

For this training, you'll explore a few options; then it will be up to you to turn off the TV and discover more.

Custom Animation Task Pane

1. Select an object on your slide that you want to animate. Click the **Animations** tab. The Custom Animation task pane will appear on your right.

2. Choose the appropriate action as follows:

▤ **Add Effect** button (this button will read "Change" once an animation has been applied). Use to animate an object. Choices include Entrance, Emphasis, Exit, and Motion Paths. When you point to either of these options, more animation choices appear.

▤ **Remove**. Use when you want to delete an animation.

▤ **Start**. Begin an animation three ways:

▤ On Click	▤ When you click the mouse, right or left keyboard arrow key, or the spacebar.
▤ With Previous	▤ Automatically with start of previous effect.
▤ After Previous	▤ Automatically when the previous effect ends.

▤ **Direction**. Some effects come in from a certain direction (e.g., the **Wipe** effect moves from left to right).

▤ **Speed**. You can change the speed of an animation from **Very Slow** to **Very Fast**.

▤ **Re-Order**. Use this to change the animation order of all or some of the animated objects you place on your slide.

▤ **Play**. Use this option to hear and/or see all your animations as they will play during your slide show.

▤ **Slide Show**. Use this to launch the slide you're working on and view as a slide show.

▤ **AutoPreview**. Tick this box so that every time you add an animation you'll see a preview of it. (To see how the animation will play in the actual slide show, click the **Slide Show** button.)

Animate Objects

Add Entrance Animation Effect

1. With an object on your slide selected, click **Add Effect** in the Custom Animation task pane (if the pane isn't in view, click the Animations tab, Custom Animation).

2. Point to **Entrance**, click **More Effects**, and double-click **Wipe** (this means that during your slide show, this object will appear on the screen using the Wipe animation).

3. Now modify the start, direction, and speed of the animation. The choices under direction and speed are obvious. With the start instruction, you can choose whether you want the animation to happen when you click your mouse or with or after a previous animation.

If you insert a picture that you want to animate, put it inside an object (see page 44) and apply the animation to the object. This way, if you decide to change the picture, you won't have to redo the animation.

Add More Effects

1. Draw more shapes and animate them. You'll see each animation in the task pane. Click different animated shapes on your slide, and watch how they become selected in the task pane (and vice versa) with the animation number next to it changing colors on the slide to indicate its selection.

2. Click the drop-down box in the Effects List next to the first animation in the Custom Animations pane. Click **Effect Options**. (Or double-click the animation.) A dialog box for that animation appears.

3. Add a sound that will play when an object enters. Click the **Effect** tab, then the **Sound** drop-down box, and choose to add a **breeze sound** (limit your use of sounds in your business presentations. I don't use these at all).

4. On the **Timing** tab under **Delay**, make at least one of your objects appear **1.5 seconds** after the others (change Start to **After Previous**); let it happen at **Medium** speed; and make it **Repeat Until Next Click**.

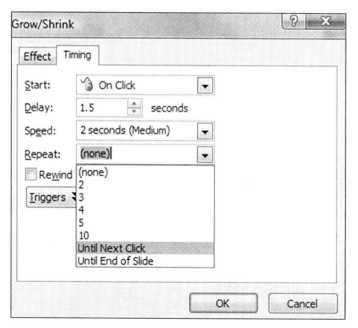

📢 *A slide transition is considered an animation so With Previous can mean with a transition.*

Delay Animations

In the previous lesson, you set an animation on one of the objects to happen After Previous, but instead of making the next animation happen right away, you delayed it by 1.5 seconds. Setting time delays means effects can overlap each other. The delay applies to the start setting of either With Previous, After Previous, or On Click. No effect has to wait to start before another finishes.

This will make much more sense once you start to create more custom animations.

Add an Exit Animation Effect

You may want an animation to happen on a shape or text when it's time for something else to appear. That's an exit animation.

1. Insert or create at least two objects on a slide, select the first one, click the **Animations** tab, **Custom Animation**.

2. Click **Add Effect** in the Custom Animation task pane, point to **Exit**, and click one of the animations.

3. Leave Start as **On Click**, and set the Speed to **Medium**.

4. Click the second object, and create an Exit animation.

5. Set Start as **With Previous**.

With this animation, when the slide opens, you'll click to make the first object appear. When you click to go to the next animation, the first object will exit as the second one appears. You can place one object on top of the other to make it appear as if the second one filled up the space of the first one.

🔊 *If you select an animated object and press **Ctrl+D**, the object and its animation will duplicate.*

Examine the Effects List

Now that you've added several custom animations to your slides, see how they're listed in the Custom Animation task pane. (Your list will differ from this graphic, but you'll use the same logic to understand what's going on.)

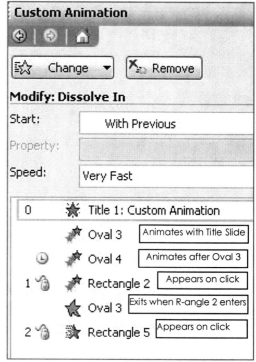

- 0, 1, 2. These numbers next to your animations (and on your slide) indicate the playing order. For example, all the animations listed with the 0 will play together (although the start of the animation could be delayed). The same applies to the animations with 1, 2, and so on. In this example, the title slide will animate With Previous (the slide transition is the thing that happens first, and the title will animate with it, and so will Oval 3).
  When you click the playing order box on the slide, the corresponding animation is highlighted in the Custom Animation task pane (and vice versa).

- A **timer** next to an animation means the Start has been set to After Previous. (Oval 4 will animate automatically after Oval 3.)

- The **mouse** indicates the animation will happen upon the next mouse click. (Rectangle 2 will animate at the next mouse click.)

The star shapes change based on the effect. If you hold your mouse over the effect, a screen tip will display the different ones that have been applied.

▤ **Green stars** indicate an Entrance effect has been applied, and the **red stars** indicate an Exit effect. (Oval 3 will exit as Rectangle 2 is coming in.)

▤ If you apply an Emphasis effect, you'll see **yellow stars**.

To summarize, the title slide will animate With Previous. The slide transition is the thing that happens first, and the title will animate with it (and so will Oval 3). Oval 4 will animate automatically after Oval 3. And Rectangle 2 will animate at the next mouse click with Oval 3 exiting at the same time.

Most people in the real world will not have time to create complicated animations. Keep everything simple and you'll be fine.

Change or Remove Animation Effects

If you ever need to change or remove an animation effect, click the object to select it, then click its animation listed in the Custom Animation task pane. To change the animation, click the **Change** button. To remove it, click the **Remove** button.

ADD A TRIGGER EFFECT

A trigger is an object such as a picture, shape, or text box on your slide that sets off an action when it's clicked. A trigger effect could be something as simple as a photo on a slide that when clicked, bulleted text appears. This effect works well for interactive presentations.

In the instructions below, you'll insert a picture as the trigger. After you click the picture, the bulleted text will enter.

1. Insert a picture onto a new slide. This picture will serve as the trigger.

2. Draw a text box 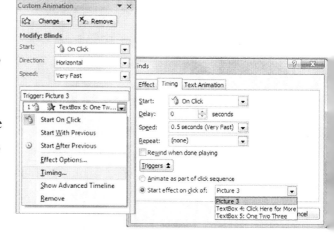 (see page 33 on how to insert a text box), move it under the picture, and type a caption in it that reads, "Click here for more information."

3. In a text placeholder (or insert another text box), type a list (does not have to be a bulleted list).

4. Create a custom animation for this list, and add an **Entrance** effect to **Start After Previous**. In the Custom Animation task pane, click the drop-down box for this effect, and click **Timing**, **Triggers**.

5. Tick **Start effect on click of**. In the drop-down menu, select the picture file you inserted to act as the trigger, click **OK**.

6. Launch your slide show, click the photo (the trigger), and your list should appear. You can animate the list to appear in different sequences.

ANIMATE PARAGRAPHS (BULLETS)

You can also add animation to any text on your slide. Add animation to the slide title using the same technique you applied to objects. If you want to animate the slide title the same way for each slide, you should change it on the master slide.

Animate Bulleted Lists

You can animate a bulleted list and have your bullets animate at once, one group at a time, or one line at a time (a build). Your presentation will probably consist of bulleted lists (paragraphs). You can animate lines of text whether they are bulleted or not.

🔊 *I usually add bullet animation to the master. As my needs change, I'll alter individual slides.*

1. Click **New Slide** on the Home tab, and choose the **Title and Content** layout.

2. Add some bulleted text with at least two levels (tab to indent bullet under at least one of the first levels).

> ▦   This is a 1st level bullet.
>
> > ▦   This is a 2nd level bullet indent.
> >
> > > ▦   This is a 3rd level bullet indent.

If you have more than one level of bulleted text, you can set each level to animate separately or together. For instance, you may want a line of bulleted text to appear with its sub-bullets, but sometimes not. You may want all the bulleted text to appear at once, but sometimes you may want to discuss each one and will display them independently. You may even want one bullet to dim as you move to the next one so your audience is focused only on the point being discussed.

3. With the placeholder surrounding the bulleted list still selected, click the **Animations** tab, and click the **Animate drop-down box**. Hold your mouse over each choice to see how it affects the bulleted list. These pre-set animations include the Fade, Wipe, and Fly In animations. Under each one of these, you can choose whether to have all bullets (considered a paragraph) appear at

once or By 1st Level Paragraph (One bullet with all its sub-bullets will appear on the screen at once.

These are not your only options. If you choose **Custom Animation,** you can choose any of the other Entrance animations (i.e., not just Fade, Wipe, and Fly In). And you'll have more choices about when the bullets should appear.

1. Click anywhere inside a bulleted list, and click the **Animations** tab, **Custom Animation.**

2. Follow the same instructions as you learned for animating objects, and add some type of Entrance effect (beginning on page 71).

3. Double-click the effect on the Effects List, click **Text Animation,** click the **Group text drop-down box** to see your options.

   ▣ **As one object.** The entire bulleted list animates at once.

   ▣ **All paragraphs at once.** Bullets on the slide will show at once.

   ▣ **By 1st level paragraphs.** One bullet with all of its sub-bullets appear at once.

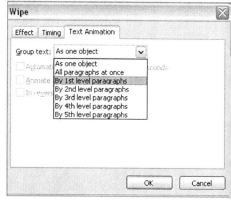

   ▣ **By 2nd level paragraphs.** When you want a bullet to appear, and with each subsequent animation, sub-bullets will appear (if it has a 3rd level indent under it, that text will appear also).

   ▣   **By 3rd level paragraphs** (and so on). If you want all three levels to show independently of each other.

Don't worry if all this seems confusing. You'll understand it more as you do it. I still have to refer back to this list.

Dim or Hide a Bullet After Discussed

To keep your audience focused on your next point, you may want to dim the previous bullet.

1. Double-click the animation in the task pane as you have before, and click the **Effect** tab in the dialog box that will appear.

2. Make each paragraph **Dim** after animation (in the **After Animation drop-down box**, choose a text color that matches the slide background as closely as possible). Or choose to **Hide on Next Mouse Click**.

Animate Lines of Text

You can use the same techniques to animate lines of text whether they're bulleted or not. You can also make them appear all at once, by word, or by letter. Follow the same instructions for animating a bulleted list. On the **Effect** tab, click the **Animate text drop-down box** and choose.

Animate Shapes as Paragraphs

You can use the same technique for animating a series of shapes as you use for bulleted and unbulleted lines of text. Draw four shapes on a slide. Now animate them just as you have with a bulleted list. Click on the first shape you want to appear during your show, and set the first shape as **By first level paragraphs**, the second shape as **By second level paragraphs**, and so on.

MOTION PATHS

A motion path is an invisible track you lay on your slide for an object to follow. For example, you can draw a star and make it move from one side of the slide to the next, then move up and off the entire slide. Motion paths offer many options for adding animation to your slide—way too many for this book.

1. Insert a shape on your slide, select it, and click the **Animations** tab, **Custom Animation**.

2. Click the **Add Effect** button, point to **Motion Paths**, and click **Turn Up Right**. (If you don't see this effect, click **More Motion Paths** to access the entire gallery. Scroll down and Look under Lines & Curves.) Click **OK** to see the effect.

Manipulate the Path

The dotted line on the slide represents the path. The green triangle on the graphic represents where the motion begins, and the red triangle indicates where it will stop. You can adjust these points.

For instance, you can make the object totally disappear off to the right during your slide show. To do this, you may have to extend the path. Click the animation (on the slide), hold your mouse over the red triangle until it turns into a two-sided arrow. Drag it until it's off the slide. Launch the show to see if you dragged it far enough.

When a path is selected, you'll see the following:

- Sizing handles (little white dots). Hold your mouse over a handle until it turns into a slanted two-headed arrow; drag it to resize.

- Rotator handle (green dot). Hold your mouse over the rotator handle, and drag the circular arrow to rotate the path.

To move the path, hold your mouse over it until it turns into a 4-headed arrow and drag. If you want to move the object and its path, select the object (not the path), and drag to the new location.

Change Effect Options

You can adjust the effect options for motion paths just as you have for custom animations. Once you're hooked, you'll spend hours exploring the possibilities. Turn off the TV, sketch what you want to make happen, and get started.

Advanced Timeline

When you start to create more complex animations, you'll want to explore using the Advanced Timeline (or timeline) to synchronize animation timings and set animation speed. The timeline shows the playing times (durations) in the form of boxes that you can drag to change. You'll be able to see other durations and can adjust them in relation to each other.

For more training on this feature, visit my Website for a demo at www.DigitalBreakthroughs.com/ppttutor.htm.

INSERT HYPERLINKS

By now, you're familiar with your mouse pointer turning into a white hand to let you know you'll be taken somewhere else when you click. You can create a hyperlink on your slides.

1. Click the Web address you typed on the blank slide, and then click the **Insert** tab, **Hyperlink** command inside the Links group.

    🔲   To link to an existing file or Web page, click Existing File or Web Page under Link to. Locate and select the file you want to link to.

    🔲   To link to a slide in your current presentation, click Place in This Document under Link to. Click the appropriate slide or custom show (you'll learn more about custom shows later).

    🔲   To link to a file that you haven't created, click Create New Document under Link to. Type a name for the new file or click **Change** to specify the path to it.

2. The Insert Hyperlink dialog box will open. The **Existing File or Web Page** instruction will be selected (if not, click it).

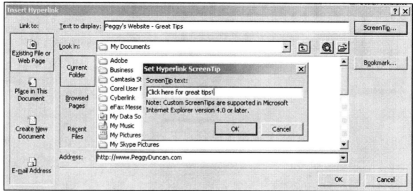

Click inside the **Address box** located near the bottom of the dialog box, and type any URL (with the http:// included).

3. Whatever appears in the **Text to display box** will be the text that will appear in your document, so type whatever you want here. In my case, I typed "Peggy's Website – Great Tips." To make the link look more professional on the slide, I'll remove the underline.

4. Assign a tip to be displayed when you rest the mouse over the hyperlink by clicking the **Screen Tip** button (upper right corner of the Insert Hyperlink dialog box), then by typing the text you want. In my case, when I hover the mouse over the link during the show, it'll read "Click here for great tips."

5. Click **OK** until you're back on your slide. To check your link, launch the slide show for that slide (**Shift+F5**). Or you can click the **Slide Show from current slide** button on the Slide Changer.

6. To view your screen tip, hold the mouse over your hyperlink while in slide show. Press **Esc** to go back to your slide.

Edit Hyperlinks

If you ever need to change the setting on a hyperlink, select the text or object, click the **Insert** tab, **Hyperlink**, **Remove link**, and create your new one.

Prevent Automatic Hyperlinks

If you don't want an email address or a Web site address to automatically turn into a live link when you type it, you can turn the feature off.

1. Click the **Office** button, **PowerPoint Options**, **Proofing**, **AutoCorrect Options**, **AutoFormat As You Type** tab.

2. Untick **Internet and network paths with hyperlinks**.

MULTIMEDIA - MUSIC, VOICE, MOVIES

You can turn your slide show into a multimedia presentation with music, your own narration, and movies. You can set PowerPoint to play sounds and music automatically or at your command.

LINKED AND EMBEDDED OBJECTS

A sound object can be either linked or embedded. A linked object is created and saved in a separate file (source), and then linked to your presentation (the destination file). Because the files are linked, when you update the source file, the destination file is also updated. But if you present on a different computer or you email the presentation to someone, the sound file will still be on *your* computer so it won't play somewhere else.

On the other hand, an embedded file is created in a separate file, and when you embed it, it becomes a part of the destination file. If you update the source file, the embedded file is not updated because they're not linked.

PowerPoint only embeds sound in the .wav format. If you have sound objects in other Windows-compatible formats and you're going to present from a different computer or email your presentation to someone, you have two options. You'll either have to convert your files to .wav so you can embed them (.wav files can get huge very quickly), or you can save all your files in one folder using Package for CD (page 109).

INSERTING SOUND FILES

To add a sound file to a presentation, it'll have to be saved in a format compatible with PowerPoint. Some of the Windows formats include:

- Windows Media Audio (wma).
- Windows Waveform (wave, wav).
- Audio Interchange File Format (aif, aiff, aifc).
- MPEG Layer 3 Audio (mp3).
- Musical Instrument Digital Interface (midi, mid, kar).

📢 *PowerPoint will only embed .wav files. All other compatible file types have to be linked. My Web site has resources for converting your files and also a link to instructions on how to trick PowerPoint into thinking an MP3 file is a .wav file. Visit www.DigitalBreakthroughs.com/ppttutor.htm.*

1. Click the **Insert** tab, **Sound**, **Sound from File**, double-click the file to insert it.

2. Choose whether you want the file to play **Automatically** or **When Clicked** (you can change this later). A sound icon will appear on your slide.

📢 *The file path to an object cannot be longer than 128 characters (e.g., c:\My Documents\Business\PSC Press\Marketing\Semi...).*

Sound Options

When you insert a sound object into your presentation, the sound icon will appear. If you double-click it, your sound will play.

To change sound options, click the icon once. A new **Options** tab will appear. You should explore the commands in the Sound Options group.

Hide the Sound Object

You can hide this sound object during your presentation by ticking **Hide During Show**.

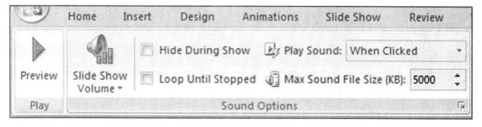

Sound – The File Size

By default, if sound files are greater than 100 kb in size, they are automatically linked to your file rather than embedded. However, PowerPoint can embed a sound file in .wav format as large as 50MB, but you'll have to change the default. Click the sound icon that appeared after you inserted a sound into your presentation. A new **Options** tab will appear. Change **Max Sound File Size (KB)** to **5000KB**, which is about 5MB. (You could go as high as 50,000KB, but embedding files this large will make your presentation file huge.)

📢 *If you use the Package for CD command, you won't have to do this because the presentation and all supporting files, regardless of the format, will be copied. For more information on Package for CD, see page 109.*

Keep Path Names Short

After many hours of frustration and research, I discovered that a movie I was inserting into PowerPoint didn't play because the path to the file was too long. The full path to the linked file has to be less than 128 characters (including the drive letter, punctuation, spaces and slashes, as in
c:\My Documents\Business\PSC Press\Marketing\Semi...).

If links are too long, not only will the media files not play, but also:

- A blank box will appear where the media file should be.

- You could receive a MMSYSTEM264 ("Not enough memory") error message when you insert the file.

- Other links in your presentation could stop working (there's a limit to the total number of characters of link information PowerPoint can store. The longer your path and file names, the sooner you reach that limit).

ADD MUSIC

You can add music and sounds from files on your computer, a network, the Internet, or the Microsoft Clip Organizer to your presentation. You can also record your own sounds to add to a presentation, or use music from a CD. The following explains various ways you can add music to spice up your presentation. (Your computer must have a sound card.)

Insert Sound Files

If you've read the information at the beginning of this chapter about linking and embedding sounds, you should have a better understanding of inserting sounds (or music). To insert a sound or music file into your presentation, click the **Insert** tab, **Sounds**, **Sound from File**, and double-click the file to insert it. Choose whether to play the music **Automatically** or **When Clicked** (you can change this later).

To change how and when the object plays inside your presentation (e.g., across a certain number slides, you'll have to use custom animation (review animating sound beginning on page 88).

Use Music from CD

If you want to play music from a CD during your show, you can set PowerPoint to play whatever CD is in your drive during your presentation (make sure you're not infringing on copyrights).

When you set this up, you don't have to put a CD in the drive because PowerPoint will play whatever CD you insert during the actual presentation. From inside the presentation and on the slide you want the music to start to play:

1. Click the **Insert** tab, **Sounds, Play CD Audio Track**.
2. Determine how much and how you want the music to play.
3. If you want music to play repeatedly until you tell it to stop, tick **Loop until stopped**. Adjust the volume by clicking the sound icon.
4. Decide if you want to hide the icon during your slide show or not.
5. After you click **OK**, choose whether to play the music **Automatically** or **When Clicked** (you can change this later).

To make any changes to your options later, click the **CD icon** that you'll see in your presentation (an Options tab will appear). Use the commands in the Set Up group to make any adjustments.

Add Animation to Sound (or Music)

You can make additional changes to how and when your music will play with custom animation. Continuing from the previous lesson, the animation will apply to whatever CD is in the drive during your presentation.

1. Click the **CD icon** to select it, and click the **Animation** tab.

2. Double-click the media object on the Custom Animation task pane, and click the **Effect**, **Timing**, and **Sound Settings** tabs to make desired adjustments.

You've learned about custom animation previously in this book. You should review this information beginning on page 68. Adding animation to sound is similar.

▤ On the **Effect tab**, you determine how much of the sound you want to hear (from the beginning, pick up where you last left off, or an exact place in the music to start). You also choose when the sound will stop (you can make it play across many slides).

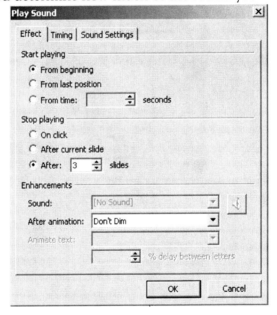

▤ On the **Timing tab**, you set the order in which the sound will play in relation to other animations in the presentation.

▤ On the **Sound Settings** tab, you can choose certain tracks from the CD to play, adjust your volume, and opt to hide the icon during your show.

Play Music Across Certain Number of Slides

After you insert the sound object, click the **CD icon** to select it, and click the **Animation** tab. Double-click the media object on the **Custom Animation** task pane (double-click the name of the file with the Play indicator to the left of it), and click the **Effect** tab. Under *Stop playing,* tick **After,** and determine how many slides you want the sound to play across.

Loop Music Continuously

If the length of your sound file isn't long enough for continuous play on a slide, you can set it up to loop (replay) until you stop it. Click the sound object on the slide, and tick **Loop Until Stopped** on the Options tab.

If you want to fade music in or out, PowerPoint can't do this. Visit my Website for resources at www.DigitalBreakthroughs.com/ppttutor.htm.

Record Narration

You can narrate portions of or the entire presentation. You'll click through your slide show as if you're giving your actual presentation, and add narrations as you go. When you get to a slide you don't want to narrate, all you have to do is be quiet. Talk only as needed, but continue to click through the presentation.

Your computer should have a sound card, speakers, and a microphone plugged in. The better the microphone, the better the sound quality.

1. Prepare your script and practice before you record.

2. Open your finished presentation. Click the **Slide Show** tab, **Record Narration** (a dialog box will appear showing you the amount of free disk space and the number of minutes you can record. Sound files can get large quickly).

3. If you haven't already tested your microphone, click **Set Microphone Level**.

4. After you set the microphone level, click **Quality** and make your selection (you'll have to research what all this means for the type of microphone you use or just use the default).

5. Tick **Link narrations in** to insert the narration as a linked object (*only if you've made the recording separately and want to play it as you click through your presentation*. If you play your presentation on a different computer, the linked file must be on the new computer. See Linked and Embedded Objects beginning on page 84). Browse to find the file to link to.

6. Click **OK** to begin recording.

7. Advance through the slide show just as you will during the actual presentation, and add narration as you go, speaking through the microphone attached to your computer. (Don't be alarmed when you don't hear other sounds you've embedded, because you can't record and play sounds at the same time.)

8. Pause during narration: If you need to pause during the narration RIGHT-click, click **Pause Narration**. To resume, RIGHT-click, click **Resume Narration**.

9. When you're finished, click **Esc**. A message will appear. To save the timings along with the narration, click Save. To save only the narration, click Don't Save.

A sound icon will appear on each slide that has narration.

▪ To listen to the sound when you're not in the show, double-click the sound icon.

▤ To change how and when the sound plays, use custom animation as explained beginning on page 88.

◀») *During the slide show, only one sound can play at a time. If you have inserted a sound that is to play automatically, it will get overridden by voice narration. Sounds that are set to play when clicked will play when you click them.*

Re-Record the Narration

If you want to change the narration on any or all slides, repeat the instructions for adding narration. If you want a new recording on a particular slide, go to that slide and re-record. The new recording will replace the old. To stop re-recording, press Esc.

Play the Narration

During your slide show, the narration will play automatically. You can turn it off before your show if you want to.

1. To run your show without narration, click the **Slide Show** tab, **Set Up Show** (or hold down the **Shift** key and click the **Slide Show from current slide** button on the Slide Changer.

2. Tick Show without narration.

Show Slide Notes for the Hearing Impaired

If you're using narration and sounds with your presentation, you should add slide notes that will appear during your presentation. For information on setting this up, see View Multiple Slides (and Notes) During Presentation on page 99.

INSERT A VIDEO

It's as easy to insert a video into your presentation as it is to insert pictures or sound. You'll need a movie file saved in a format compatible with PowerPoint. The best compatibility test is to try opening the movie with the Windows Media Player. If it plays, it will work with PowerPoint as well.

Some of the PC formats include:

- Windows Media Video (wmv).

- Audio Video Interleave (avi).

- QuickTime (mov), but you may have problems.

(I have a list of resources on my Web site you can use to convert videos at www.DigitalBreakthroughs.com/ppttutor.htm.)

1. In Normal view, click the **Insert** tab, **Movie** drop down, **Movie from File** if you have one (if not, click Movie from Clip Organizer to locate movies that may have come with your software. More information on using the Clip Organizer is on page 27).

2. **Browse** to find your file, and double-click it to insert it onto your slide. Choose whether to play it **Automatically** or **When Clicked** (you can change this later).

3. Launch your slide show to view your movie (**Shift+F5**).

Dress Your Slide for the Movie

Instead of placing your video on a slide as a plain object, dress it up using shapes, photos, etc. In the image below, I inserted a shape and dressed it using a beveled edge with a glow effect and a text box for the verbiage. I dragged the actual video to the middle.

Change How Movie Plays

After you insert a movie, you can change how it plays by using the custom animation command as you have in previous lessons. If you choose to play the movie automatically, the first animation is the Play setting. The Trigger (the action that happens when the movie is clicked during the show) is set to Pause (clicking the movie

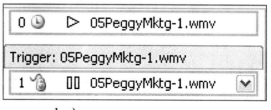

again during the show will resume play).

When you click the Add Effect or Change button, you'll see other animation options.

Play Movie Across Several Slides

1. Continuing with the Custom Animation pane open, click to select the video on the slide, **Options** tab, **Play Movie** drop down box, **Play across slides**.

2. Go to the Custom Animation pane, and double-click the box with the movie name (has the triangle which indicates play).

3. Keep the movie playing for several slides. Under **Stop playing**, **After** should be ticked. Type the total number of slides you want the file to play across.

4. Click the **Timing** tab, and **Delay** the start of the movie by 3 seconds (for this example).

5. Click the **Movie Settings** tab, and decide if you want the movie to hide while playing or zoom to full screen.

If the movie is long enough, and you want it to play through the entire presentation, type 999 in the After box.

Change When Movie Plays

If you change your mind about how a movie will play in Show mode, click the video object to select it, **Options** tab, and choose in the **Play Movie** list.

Play Movie Continuously

If you want a movie to keep playing until you stop it, click the video to select it, **Options** tab, tick **Loop Until Stopped**.

Insert the Windows Media Player

You can insert the Windows Media Player onto a slide and assign a movie to it. During your slide show, you'll be able to adjust the movie volume, stop it, etc. (the free player must be installed on your computer).

1. Add the Developer tab to the ribbon (click the **Office** button, **PowerPoint Options, Popular,** tick **Show Developer tab in the Ribbon, OK**).

2. Click the **Developer** tab, **More Controls**. Scroll to and click **Windows Media Player, OK,** click and drag on the slide to draw it. Resize from the corners if you need to.

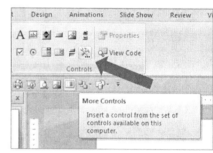

3. Add the movie (RIGHT-click on the player, **Properties**. You should be on the **Alphabetic** tab. Double-click **(Custom)**, **Browse** to find the file, and double-click it.)

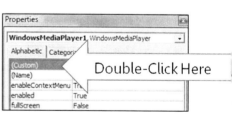

4. Close the Properties dialog box, and launch your slide show, **OK**.

Insert a Video from YouTube

If you're going to be connected to the Internet during your presentation, you can add a YouTube video and play it right from PowerPoint.

1. Go to **www.Youtube.com,** and find the video you want to insert. Copy the URL (to find the URL, go to the video you want and click the **Share** link under the video).

2. Back in PowerPoint, click the **Developer** tab (refer to the lesson on inserting the Windows Media Player if you don't have this tab), **More Controls.** Scroll to click **Shock Wave Flash Object, OK.** Click and drag on the slide to draw it. Resize from the corners if you need to.

3. RIGHT-click on the object, **Properties.** You should be on the **Alphabetic** tab. Next to **Movie,** paste the URL of the YouTube video.

   In the URL, delete **watch?.** Then replace the = sign with a slash /.

   If you don't want your video to **Loop,** change to False. If you don't want your video to start playing right away, change **Playing** to False.

4. Close the Properties dialog box, and launch your slide show. Remember, having used this method to insert the video, you'll need to have a live Internet connection to play it.

📢⁾⁾ *Visit www.Digitalbreakthroughs.com/ppttutor.htm for a link to a demo video.*

Insert a Flash (FLV) Video

Inserting a Flash video on a PowerPoint slide is very similar to inserting a YouTube video.

1. Follow the same instructions for inserting the Shock Wave Flash Object as explained for inserting a YouTube video. Then RIGHT-click on the object, **Properties**.

2. Add the entire path to (e.g., C:/...) and filename of your video on the **Movie** line. On the **EmbedMovie** line, make sure it reads *True* (this ensures the Flash file is saved with the presentation).

3. Close the Properties box, and launch your slide show.

📢⁾ *Visit www.Digitalbreakthroughs.com/ppttutor.htm for a link to a demo video.*

THE SHOW

VIEWING THE PRESENTATION

Edit Presentation While You View the Changes

When I'm working on a PowerPoint presentation, I like seeing it in Show mode as I create or edit it (the following will make sense if you use dual monitors. I have a second monitor connected to my laptop).

Open a presentation, and press **F5** to start the show. If the show appears on the same monitor you opened it on, change your settings. In Normal view, click the **Slide Show** tab. In the Monitors group, click the drop down next to Show Presentation On:, choose your additional monitor, and press **F5** again. You can now edit your presentation on one monitor, and view it as a show on the other simultaneously.

View Multiple Slides (and Notes) During Presentation

Presenter View allows you to run your presentation on one monitor but have your audience look at something different on another monitor (or projection screen). You'll see more of your presentation details such as speaker notes, upcoming slides, the time, and more. Your audience will only see the current slide (or you can set it up so they can see the slide with speaker notes (e.g., for the hearing impaired).

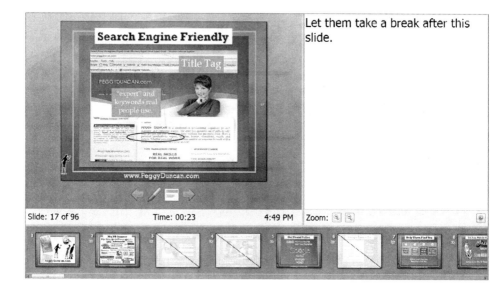

1. In Normal view, click the **Slide Show** tab, and click **Use Presenter View** located in the Monitors group.

2. Press **F5** to launch your show to see the results (if you use two monitors or when you're connected to a projector).

If your presentation has sound, such as narration, the hearing impaired can view your presentation and read your slide notes if you have them. In the Monitors group, choose which monitor to ***Show Presentation On****.*

NAVIGATE DURING A SHOW

Now that your presentation and handouts look great, you'll want to look like a pro as you're giving your presentation. Try the following.

Navigation Tips for the Slide Show

- Press **F5** to launch your slide show from the beginning if you're in Normal or Slide Sorter view.

- Refer back to a certain slide. If you know the page number of the slide you want to go to, type the slide number, and press **Enter**. (Also use: **N**=Next, **P**=Previous, spacebar, arrow keys.)

- Go to a particular slide, but you don't know the page number. Press **Ctrl+S** during your slide show for a listing of slides. Double-click the one you want to go to.

- Go to the first slide by briefly holding down both mouse buttons simultaneously.

- Keep your audience focused on you during a discussion. Type **W** (or a comma) to turn your screen white. Or type **B** (or a period) for black. Type W (or B) again to continue the presentation.

- Stop the show by pressing **Esc**.

Make Notes During Slide Show

You can make markings on the screen during your presentation.

1. RIGHT-click anywhere on the screen during your presentation, point to **Pointer Options**, make your selection.
2. Mark directly on the screen.
3. Press **Esc** to cancel the pointer.
4. Press **E** to erase all markings.

Rehearse Timing

1. In Normal view, click the **Slide Show** tab, **Rehearse Timings**.
2. Rehearse your presentation and go through each slide just as you will during the actual presentation. If you need to pause, click the Pause button on the Rehearsal toolbar. Press **Esc** when finished.

Self-Navigating Show

You can set your slide show up to run continuously on its own.

1. Click the **Slide Show** tab, **Set Up Show**. Tick **Loop continuously until 'Esc'**. This slide show will loop continuously until stopped, and slides will advance using timings you set with transitions (see page 68).

2. To stop the show, press **Esc**.

Create a Kiosk

You can set your show up as a kiosk and "disconnect" the keyboard and mouse clicks that PowerPoint normally uses to progress to the next slide during a show (i.e., in kiosk mode, the viewer will not be able to click a mouse arrow key to advance to the next slide).

You can set the slides up to advance based on your transition timings, or the user can advance the slides as desired. If it's the latter, you'll have to create action buttons (page 48) and hyperlinks (page 82) that make it obvious what the user needs to do (e.g., Click Here or a Home button). The user will be able to click them to progress to other slides, Websites, etc. They will not be able to use the mouse to advance without these.

1. Use what you've already learned about creating action buttons and hyperlinks to create on-screen navigation for your show.

2. Click the **Slide Show** tab, and click **Set Up Slide Show**.

3. Set your show to be Browsed at a kiosk (full screen).

Once your show is set up as a kiosk, the user will use your action buttons, hyperlinks, and command buttons to progress to other slides, but not the keyboard or mouse as they normally would.

You should pay close attention to the flow of your kiosk presentation and test it out on a few users before you take it public. If a user should click something on a slide, it needs to be obvious.

Never leave them hanging or guessing what to do next. For example, if you provide a button for the user to click to another slide, will they know what to do when it's time to leave that slide and go to another? Do you need a Back button, a Help button, Continue arrow, etc.? And when they've finished, have you told them how to end?

Run and Update Web Pages During Show

If you need to display Web pages (or documents on your local drive) and refresh them in real-time during your slide show, check out the resources at www.DigitalBreakthroughs.com/ppttutor.htm.

CUSTOM SLIDE SHOW

If you have a presentation that you want to produce condensed or different versions of, you won't have to create another file. You can create a custom show.

Custom shows are variations of a show that reside inside the original file. They work great if you present to different people, and perhaps the first few pages of your presentation are always the same, but other parts are different. You can create custom shows from inside your original presentation, and hyperlink to any of them.

Create a Custom Show

1. From Normal view, click the **Slide Show** tab, click the **Custom Slide Show** drop-down box, and click **Custom Shows, New,** name the show in the name box.

2. Hold down the Ctrl key and click to select the slides you want to add to the custom show, click **Add, OK, Show** (to see the show), or **Close.**

View the Custom Show Later

1. Open the original file from which you built the custom show.

2. Click **F5** to start your show from the beginning.

3. During the show, RIGHT-click, and click **Custom Show**, and click the custom show you created.

4. (Or, from Normal view, click the **Slide Show** tab, **Custom Shows**, click the custom show.)

Create a Hyperlink to the Custom Show

Suppose you're doing several presentations to different groups. The first few pages of your presentation are the same for each, but later in the presentation, you need to hyperlink to pages for a different audience.

1. Select the text or drawing object you want to display as the hyperlink, and then click the **Insert** tab, **Hyperlink** (or click the **Hyperlink** command).

2. Under Link to:, click **Place in This Document**. At the bottom of the list, you'll see **Custom Shows**. Make sure you scroll down far enough to see all the custom shows you've created. Click the appropriate one.
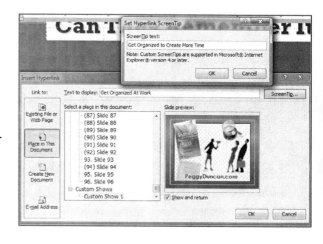

3. You can assign a tip to be displayed when you rest the mouse over the hyperlink (after you launch the show) by clicking **Screen Tip**, and then typing the text you want.

If you'll want to return to the page with the hyperlink after viewing the custom show, tick **Show and Return**, **OK**.

Launch your slide show (**F5**), and test your links. Hold the mouse over your hyperlink, read the screen tip if you created one, and click.

Hide Slides

Custom shows work well if you have different versions of a presentation for different audiences. However, I use a wireless mouse when I present so I'm all over the room. If I know I won't be close enough to my laptop to click a hyperlink, I won't use custom shows. Instead, I have all my slides on a topic in one presentation and hide and unhide slides as needed (in Slide Sorter view, RIGHT-click any slide, click **Hide**. Repeat the steps to unhide).

SAVING FILES

SAVE PRESENTATION AS A SHOW

You can save your presentation as a Show out on your Windows Desktop. When you're ready to present, simply double-click the Show file, and your slide show will start automatically. You won't have to open PowerPoint, find the file, open it, start the show.

1. Click the **Office** button, **Save As.** Choose to save on the **Desktop**.

2. At the bottom of the dialog box, click the **Save as type** box, and scroll to choose **PowerPoint Show (*.ppsx)**.

3. Password-protect the file (if you want to prevent people from making changes). Click the **Tools** button drop-down box in the lower right corner of the Save As dialog box (next to the Save button), **General Options**. Add a password that's easy for you to remember.

4. To launch your Show, double-click it.

📢 *Later, if you need to make changes to your presentation, open the file (.pptx) in PowerPoint as you normally would, not the Show (.ppsx). Resave as .ppsx when finished.*

SAVE A SLIDE AS A PICTURE

When I need a business card, postcard, Twitter background, etc., I create it in PowerPoint and save the slide as a jpeg. The first thing I'll do is resize the slide to the size of the finished piece. For example, if you create a postcard that's 6x4 inches, click the **Design** tab, **Page Setup**, change the width and height, and tick **Landscape**.

📢 *If the design bleeds off the edges of the card, change the size to 6.13 x 4.13 so when the printer cuts the card, you won't have white edges.*

Design and save your slide as you normally would. When you're ready to save the slide as a picture, click the **Office** button, **Save As**, choose the desired graphic format (e.g., JPEG), in the **Save as type** list, and click **Save**.

Save Slide in Higher Resolution

Native PowerPoint saves a slide as a picture in 96dpi resolution. This is fine if you're posting the graphic to the Web, but it's not high enough to send to a print vendor. For a solution that will allow you to bump up the resolution to say 300dpi, visit my Web site at www.DigitalBreakthroughs.com/ppttutor.htm.

Email a Single Slide

If you need to email a single slide, go to that slide, and click to save the presentation as a picture (.jpg). Click to save the **Current Slide Only**, then email the file.

Another option is to go to Slide Sorter view, click the slide to select it, and press **Ctrl+C** to copy the slide you want to email. Create a new presentation, go to Slide Sorter view, and press **Ctrl+V** to paste it. Name the file and email it as you normally would.

Post Slides on the Web

You can post slideshows on the Web and offer them to the public or via a secret URL. Visit www.Slideshare.net, and set up a free account.

REDUCE FILE SIZE

If a PowerPoint file size seems to increase for no reason, you can reduce the file size by up to 50 percent by resaving it under a different name. If doing this once doesn't work, try it again.

Compress Pictures to Make File Smaller

If you've inserted a lot of pictures using the Insert Picture command, you can make your file smaller by compressing the picture file sizes (I usually resize photos before I insert them into PowerPoint).

You can compress one picture or all of them at once. If you choose to compress all pictures, wait until you have inserted all of them so PowerPoint won't attempt to re-compress them. (This doesn't work with pictures that are pasted in as opposed to inserted with the Insert Picture command.)

1. Click on the picture you want to compress or if you want to compress all pictures, click on any one. A **Format** tab will appear, and it's already active.

2. Click the **Compress Pictures** command located in the Adjust group, and make desired selections.

If your file size doesn't shrink after you do the compress, resave the file under a different name.

PACKAGE FOR CD

Package for CD eliminates any issues if you plan to play your presentation with music, etc., on another computer. It allows you to copy one or more presentations along with supporting files (including linked files such as sound) onto something portable such as a CD or Flash drive (or to its own folder). The PowerPoint Viewer, which enables users to view PowerPoint even if it's not installed on their computer, is included by default. You can also add other files to the presentation package, and you can opt to embed TrueType fonts.

If you don't use the Package for CD command, you'll have to manually save all the files you're using in a presentation into the same folder. If you play your presentation on another computer, you'll have to take everything in the entire folder.

📢 *If you save your files onto a rewritable CD (CD-RW), the existing content will be overwritten. Use the less expensive CDR.*

1. Click the **Office** button, point to **Publish**, click **Package for CD**, give the file a short name with no space.

2. Click to **Add Files** you need (PowerPoint chooses the linked and embedded files on its own so no need to add these. If you have more than one presentation linked, click Add Files).

   Files will play in the order they're saved, so click to re-order if needed.

3. Click **Options**, and make necessary changes. Click **OK, Copy to CD** (or Copy to Folder).

📢 *Under **Options**, tick **Embedded TrueType fonts** to ensure your presentation will show properly. Fonts with built-in copyrights cannot be packaged. You are not limited to copying files to a CD although that's what the name implies.*

If you experience a problem with PowerPoint not recognizing your burner, click **Copy to Folder** instead of Copy to CD, then burn the files to CD as you normally would. If you Package for CD onto a rewritable CD (CD-RW), the existing content will be overwritten.

Password-Protect Your CD

You can protect content on the CD by adding passwords when you Package for CD.

For presentations that require more security, you can add Information Rights Management (IRM). IRM helps prevent sensitive documents or email messages from being copied, forwarded, or edited by unauthorized people.

Presentations protected by Information Rights Management cannot be viewed in the PowerPoint Viewer. (Check PowerPoint Help for more information on IRM.)

Make Presentation Read-Only

Click the **Office** button, **Prepare**, **Mark as Final**.

Embed Fonts in the File

If you don't use the Package for CD command, be sure to use the Embed Fonts in the File command. I always back up my presentation onto a USB flash drive. If I ever have to use someone else's computer on the fly, I'll at least know that my fonts will not be substituted on the target machine. If you've ever seen your text or bullets turn into something weird, you'll know what I mean.

Whether you have already saved the presentation or not, the steps work the same.

1. From inside the presentation, click the **Office** button, **Save As**.

2. Click the **Tools** button drop-down box in the lower right corner of the Save As dialog box (next to the Save button), **Save Options**.

3. Tick **Embed fonts in the file**, and continue saving as you normally would.

📣 *I also do this with any template I create. This way, it's already in place with every presentation based on that template.*

Create an Autorun CD

By default, when you Package for CD, the CD is set up to play all presentations automatically in the order you specify, or autorun. You can change this default setting to automatically play only the first presentation, to automatically display a dialog box from which people can select the presentations they want to play, or to disable the automatic features and require people to manually start the CD.

Click **Options** in the Package for CD process for these commands.

CREATE HANDOUTS

When you create a handout of your presentation, you have the choice of doing it from PowerPoint, or you can send your presentation to Word and use its powerful formatting features.

In addition to being a computer trainer, I'm a professional organizer and have helped many people remove clutter and create order in their offices. I can't begin to tell you how many useless presentation handouts I've helped trash. I've seen handouts as much as 1-inch thick...handouts that were never looked at again. And in color!

Save trees and your company some money and consider keeping everything simple, printing in black and white, several slides to a page (make sure it's readable), and only printing the pages people will really need.

1. Click the **Office** button, **Print, Print.** Study the resulting dialog box for your different options.

2. Choose **Handouts** in the **Print what** box. You may rarely need to print the more expensive color handouts, so for Color/Grayscale, choose **Pure Black and White**.

   (If you ever want to see how your presentation will look in black and white from inside PowerPoint, click the View tab and click one of the options in the Color/Grayscale group).

3. Choose to print 3 **Slides per page**.

VIEW NOTES PAGES

You may have typed private notes in the notes pane under your slides. If you need to view them, go to Normal view, and click the **View** tab, **Notes Pages**.

Format Notes Pages

If you'd like to format the font on your Notes Pages, click the **View** tab, **Notes Master**, select the text (e.g., Header), and make desired changes.

Print Notes Pages

To print notes pages, choose **Notes Pages** in the **Print what** drop-down box located in the Print dialog box. If you added text in the header and footer of the notes pages (described beginning on page 15), it will print also.

Create a Slide List

If you need a list of your slides, print your presentation as you normally would, but in the *Print What* box, choose **Outline**.

Print Preview

You can preview how your presentation will look when printed with the Print Preview command. While in preview mode, you can click to choose which format to print, change color mode, and more. Click the **Office** button, **Print**, **Print Preview** (or click the Print Preview command on the Quick Access Toolbar). Click **Close** when finished or print from this screen.

Create a Handout in Word

If you send your handout to Word, you'll have more options for formatting (e.g., a more extensive header and footer), and the handout layout (e.g., print your slide with your notes beside it). But even if you change your presentation to black and white in PowerPoint, it will still come into Word in color!

1. Click the **Office** button, **Publish, Create Handouts in Microsoft Office Word** (if it's installed on your computer), choose your layout option. For now, choose the most common, Blank lines next to slides.

   The Paste option will be ticked. If you choose Paste Link, every time you make a change in your PowerPoint presentation, the change will be reflected in your Word handout. With Paste Link, as you add changes to your slides, you may have to close the Word document and reopen it to see the changes. When you double-click the linked slide in Word, it'll open in PowerPoint.

   For now, leave this as **Paste**, but come back later to play with the Paste Link command.

2. (Your handout will come into Word formatted as a table). Click the **Insert** tab, and add a Header and Footer with your contact information, company logo, page number, etc., just as you would a regular Word document.

3. Create a PDF of handout. Once I create my handout, I use Adobe Acrobat (full version) to create a black and white PDF. This is what I'll send to my client for copies.

Tips on Presenting

- Spend more time planning your presentation than creating it.

- Don't get caught up in the technology and lose sight of your message.

- Simple is better. Use the same slide transitions and bullet, text animation throughout as much as possible.

- Enhance your presentation with photos or some type of graphic element on about every 3rd slide (more if you can make it work).

- Text size should be no smaller than 18 pt for readability at a distance, but starting at 32 pt is even better.

- Keep text to a minimum, six lines per slide, and six words per line.

- Use no more than three typefaces per slide. You don't want your slides to resemble a ransom note.

- Do not overuse all caps. The human eye is accustomed to going up and down when reading.

- Use the professionally-designed themes that come with the software if you're not sure what matches. Or create your own design that resembles your Web site and brand.

- Spell check to maintain credibility. If words are wrong, audience won't trust your numbers.

- Use dark background and bright text if preparing on-screen show.

- Spend no more than 2-3 minutes presenting each slide. If you read your slides, they could have stayed home and reviewed your handout.

- During offline discussions, blacken or whiten the screen.

- Always take a no- or low-tech backup (e.g., Flash drive, paper).

- Videotape your performance to improve techniques.

- Interject humor as appropriate to keep presentation lively.

INDEX

POWERPOINT SHORTCUT KEYS

When you hold your mouse over a toolbar button, it displays a tool tip to let you know what happens when you click the button.

Text Formatting

Increase Font Size	CTRL+]
Decrease Font Size	CTRL+[
Center Paragraph	CTRL+E
Justify Paragraph	CTRL+J
Left-Align Paragraph	CTRL+L
Right-Align Paragraph	CTRL+R
Change Case	Shift+F3 and toggle to what you want
Create Hyperlink	CTRL+K

Deleting and Copying

Undo	CTRL+Z
Redo	CTRL+Y
Copy by Dragging	Select then CTRL as you drag

Navigating in Text Blocks

End of Line	END
Beginning of Line	HOME
Paragraph Up	CTRL+Up Arrow
Paragraph Down	CTRL+Down Arrow
Go to End of Presentation	CTRL+END
Go to Start of Presentation	CTRL+HOME

Navigating and Working With Objects

To Previous Object	Shift + TAB
To Next Object	TAB (comes in especially handy when you're trying to select tiny objects that you can't grab with your mouse)
Select Entire Document	CTRL+A
Drag and Drop Copy	CTRL, select it and Drag
Create a Duplicate Object	Select it and CTRL+D

Selecting Text

Select All	CTRL+A or F2
Select Any Text	Drag with left mouse button depressed
Select Word	Double-Click
Select Paragraph	Triple-Click
Drag and Drop	Select and Drag
Drag and Drop Copy	CTRL+Select and Drag

Developing Slides

New Presentation	CTRL+N
Save	CTRL+S, F12
Save As	F12
Print	CTRL+P
Find	CTRL+F
Replace	CTRL+H
New Slide with layout choices	CTRL+M
New Slide just like last layout	Shift+CTRL+M
Exit/Quit	CTRL+Q or ALT+F4

Drawing and Formatting

Guides: Show/Hide (toggle)	ALT+F9
Guides: Create Multiple	CTRL+Drag any Guide
Grid/Guide Release Snap Temporarily	ALT as you drag
Switch from Normal View to Master View	Shift+Click Normal View Button
Group	CTRL+Shift+G
Ungroup	CTRL+Shift+H
Regroup	CTRL+Shift+J
Nudge object	Arrow Key
Nudge object smaller increment	CTRL+Arrow Key

Slide Show - During

Go to Slide <number>	<number> Enter
Go to Last Slide During Show	END
Black/Unblack Screen	B or Period
White/Unwhite Screen	W or Comma
End Show	ESC, Minus
Erase Screen Annotations	E
Advance to Hidden Slide	H (only if hidden slide is next to the one you're on)
Advance to Next Slide	Mouse Click, Spacebar, N, Right Arrow, Down Arrow, Page Down
Return to Previous Slide	Backspace, P, Left Arrow, Up Arrow, Page Up
Show All Slides	Ctrl+S (double-click the slide you want to Go To)

PEGGY DUNCAN

Peggy Duncan is an award-winning personal productivity expert, speaker, consultant, coach, and author. She travels internationally helping busy people spend less time working but get more done. In September 2009, she founded a productivity and training center, **The Digital Breakthroughs Institute**, offering one-day workshops for business people.

Her other books include *The Time Management Memory Jogger™* and *Conquer Email Overload with Better Habits, Etiquette, and Outlook 2007*. Three booklets include *Get Organized at Work and Make It Easy, Shameless Self-Promotion: Do-It-Yourself SEO (search engine optimization,* and *Up to Speed on Your BlackBerry®*. More information is at www.PeggyDuncan.com/learnmore.htm.

Peggy is an award-winning technology blogger, **www.SuiteMinute.com**. She has appeared on CNN, TODAY, ABC News, PBS, and Black Enterprise Business Report. Her expertise has been cited in O-The Oprah Magazine, Entrepreneur, SUCCESS, Real Simple, Health, Fitness, Black Enterprise, Self, Essence, Good Housekeeping, PINK, Positive Thinking, Woman's World, Men's Health, The New York Times, The Wall Street Journal, The Washington Post, and The International Herald Tribune.

"I love the way you find new tricks that I never would have had time to discover on my own."
Carolyn Pund, CMP, CMM
Global Meetings & Events Manager

The Durham, NC native received a BBA degree in marketing and a train the trainer certification from Georgia State University in Atlanta, Georgia. She was formally trained at IBM and was recognized by the chairman for streamlining processes that saved the company close to a million dollars a year.

Connect at 404-492-8197, worksmart@peggyduncan.com, Twitter.com/peggyduncan.

www.**DigitalBreakThroughs**.com

Yes! Peggy Duncan is available to train your team on land, at sea, and on the Web.
At her place or yours.
worksmart@PeggyDuncan.com - 404-492-8197 Eastern

Instead of hiring someone who read a book or bought a CD and learned a script, hire a trainer who sits with busy people helping them figure out a better way to work. Hire someone who can help them examine and improve every aspect of how they work because she's a combination professional organizer, project manager, and computer trainer. Hire someone whose business is totally focused on helping professionals spend less time working but get more done.

Productivity

Find Time to Lead

Get Organized So You Can Think!

Spend Less Time Working but Get More Done

Technology

Computer Magic! Finish Work Six Times Quicker

Conquer Email Overload and Manage Your Time with Outlook

PowerPoint Advanced (Create Marketing Collateral)

Web 2.0

Do-It-Yourself Search Engine Optimization

WordPress Blogging Bootcamp

Also Offering Training Open to the Public
www.**DigitalBreakThroughs**.com

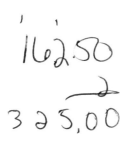

$$162.50$$
$$\times 2$$
$$325.00$$

CPSIA information can be obtained at www.ICGtesting.com
Printed in the USA
267447BV00001B/54/P

9 780967 472881